INVASION
OF
OTHER GODS

INVASION
OF
OTHER GODS

Protecting Your Family
from the Seduction
of the New Spirituality

by

David Jeremiah with
Carole C. Carlson

WORD PUBLISHING
Dallas·London·Vancouver·Melbourne

INVASION OF OTHER GODS
THE SEDUCTION OF NEW AGE SPIRITUALITY

Unless otherwise indicated, all Scripture references are from the New King James Version of the Bible, copyright © 1979, 1980, 1982, 1990, Thomas Nelson, Inc., Publisher. Used by permission.

Scriptures indicated NIV are from The Holy Bible, New International Version. Copyright ©1973, 1978, 1984, International Bible Society. Used by permission of Zondervan Bible Publishers.

Scriptures indicated TLB are from The Living Bible, copyright © 1971 by Tyndale House Publishers, Wheaton, Illinois.

Other Scripture verses are from *The Message*, copyright © 1993. Used by permission of NavPress Publishing Group.

Personal stories and anecdotes included in this volume are based on fact; however, in some cases details have been changed to protect identities.

Library of Congress Cataloging-in-Publication Data:

Jeremiah, David.
    Invasion of other gods: the seduction of new age spirituality/David Jeremiah with C. C. Carlson.
        p.   cm.
    Includes bibliographical references.
    ISBN 0–8499–3987–9 (trade paper)
    1. Family—Religious life.   2. New Age movement—Controversial literature.   3. Occultism—Controversial literature.   4. Occultism—Religious aspects—Christianity.   I. Carlson, Carole C.   II. Title.
BV4526.2.J47   1995
239'.9—dc20   94–44250
                                                                              CIP

890129 QKP 9876543

Printed in the United States of America.

To Lowell Davey . . . who throughout his life has been committed to standing for the truth of God's Word . . . who turned his passion for evangelism into the Bible Broadcasting Network, a group of more than thirty stations that present the good news of the gospel twenty-four hours a day.

CONTENTS

ACKNOWLEDGMENTS

A special thanks to the following people for their important contributions to this project: Steve Bell (Concerts in Prayer), Helen and Karin Bernhardt, Eric Buehrer, Don Cardenas (Promise Keepers), Dr. Paul Cedar, Christian Research Institute, Dr. Ann Croissant, Dr. Chuck Emert, Paul Joiner, Janice Lyons, the Rev. Roland Murphy, Dr. Samuel Nandakumar, the Spiritual Counterfeits Project, Glenda Parker, Kay Parker (National Day of Prayer), Probe Ministries, John Weldon, and Carrie Urban.

And an extra-special thanks to:

Our agents, Tom Thompson and Sealy Yates, who believed in this project.

Kip Jordon, Joey Paul, and Nancy Norris at Word, who were patient with us.

Sue Ann Jones for her editing skills.

Bob and Gretchen Passantino, who gave us their expertise with research and information.

Donna Jeremiah and Ward Carlson, who were constant sources of love, encouragement, and coffee.

You shall have no other gods before Me. You shall not make for yourself a carved image—any likeness of anything that is in heaven above, or that is in the earth beneath, or that is in the water under the earth; you shall not bow down to them nor serve them. For I, the LORD your God, am a jealous God.

Exodus 20:3–5

INTRODUCTION

O̲ur A̲merican c̲ulture i̲s b̲eing s̲haped by subversive forces. While we fight crime in the streets and corruption in high places the enemy has slipped in the back door and turned off the alarm system.

In a desperate search for spiritual significance, many people, including Christians, have been led into the territory of "other gods" without understanding the danger.

The story of one woman whose spiritual odyssey was described in *Newsweek* illustrates the longing of those who are searching for meaning in a topsy-turvy world.

Rita McClain's spiritual journey began in Iowa, where she grew up in the fundamentalist world of the Pentecostal Church. What she remembers most about that time are tent meetings and an overwhelming feeling of guilt. In her 20s she tried less doctrinaire Protestantism. That, too, proved unsatisfying. By the age of 27, McClain had rejected all organized religion. "I really felt like a pretty wounded Christian," she says. For the next 18 years, she sought inner peace only in nature, through rock climbing in the mountains or hiking in the desert. That seemed enough.

Then, six years ago, in the aftermath of an emotionally draining divorce, McClain's spiritual life blossomed.

3

Just as she had once explored mountains, she began scouting the inner landscape. She started with Unity, a metaphysical church near her Marin County, California, home. It was a revelation, light-years away from the "Old Testament kind of thing I knew very well from my childhood." The next stop was Native American spiritual practices. Then it was Buddhism at Marin County's Spirit Rock Meditation Center, where she has attended a number of retreats, including one that required eight days of silence.

These disparate rituals melded into a personal religion, which McClain, a 50-year-old nurse, celebrates at an ever-changing altar in her home. Right now the altar consists of an angel statue, a small bottle of "sacred water" blessed at a women's vigil, a crystal ball, a pyramid, a small brass image of Buddha sitting on a brass leaf, a votive candle, a Hebrew prayer, a tiny Native American basket from the 1850s and a picture of her "most sacred place," a madrone tree near her home.[1]

Rita's journey has taken her from the worship of the one true God of the Bible to the daily bowing down before nine different gods.

Neo-pagan practices such as higher consciousness, crystals, karma, past-life therapy, and the healing of memories, together with their gurus, spirit guides, universal forces, and higher powers, have infiltrated Main Street. Dissatisfaction with the materialism of the modern world and anxiety over the coming millennium have driven sincere seekers outside their own cultures to explore the other gods of the occult.

And what is happening to us today has happened before. The prophet Isaiah, seven centuries before Christ, spoke out against the other gods of his day. The kingdom of Judah, to which he ministered, was wallowing in the corruptions of bribery, murder, and lewdness. Idolatry was practiced everywhere. But here's the paradox: "When Israel fell into idolatry, it did not openly renounce the worship of the God of Abraham, Isaac, and Jacob in order to bow before the pagan shrines. Rather, the nation combined the old rituals with what it knew of the Canaanite religion."[2]

We learn how vile the perverted worship of Judah had become when we read what happened when godly Josiah became king and began to restore the purity of Jehovah-worship. Watch what he had to do to accomplish that objective:

- He brought out of the temple all the articles that were made for Baal and Asherah (the gods of the Assyrians) and for the hosts of heaven, and he burned them outside Jerusalem in the fields of Kidron and carried the ashes to Bethel (see 2 Kings 23:4).

- He removed the idolatrous priests whom the kings of Judah had ordained to burn incense on the high places in the city of Jerusalem, and those who burned incense to Baal, to the sun, to the moon, to the constellations, and to all the hosts of heaven (see 2 Kings 23:5).

- He brought out the wooden image from the house of the Lord to the Brook Kidron outside Jerusalem, burned it in the Brook Kidron, ground it to ashes, and threw the ashes on the graves of the common people (see 2 Kings 23:6).

- He tore down the ritual booths of the perverted persons who were practicing sodomy and prostitution in religious rituals (see 2 Kings 23:7).

- He killed those who consulted mediums and spiritists (see 2 Kings 23:7).

About one hundred years later when Ezekiel was ministering to the exiled Jews, the same thing happened again. On one occasion, the Lord gave Ezekiel a vision that miraculously transported him to the door of the north gate of the inner court of Jerusalem. Ezekiel was confronted by an image that had been placed there by wicked King Manasseh. The Bible describes the image as "the Seat of Jealousy." Most scholars believe that "the Seat of Jealousy" was an image of the Syrian mother-goddess Asherah (see 2 Kings 21:1–7 and 2 Chron. 33:7).

> [The Lord spoke again to Ezekiel and said:] "Son of man, lift your eyes now toward the north." So I lifted my eyes toward the north, and there, north of the altar gate, was this image of jealousy in the entrance. (Ezek. 8:5)

In two places in the temple of God, pagan idols had been set up for worship. But that's not the worst of it. Keep reading. Ezekiel is now brought to a door of the court where there was a hole in the wall. When Ezekiel dug into the hole in the wall, there was a door, and when he went through the door he saw every sort of creeping thing, abominable beasts, and all the idols of the house of Israel portrayed all around on the walls (see Ezek. 8:10).

And standing before those images were seventy men of the elders of Israel. Each man had a censer in his hand, and a thick cloud of incense ascended.

Then the Lord took Ezekiel to the north gate of the Lord's house and showed him women sitting there, weeping for Tammuz, the Babylonian nature god (see Ezek. 8:14).

Then the Lord took Ezekiel into the inner court of the Lord's house.

> And there, at the door of the temple of the LORD, between the porch and the altar, were about twenty-five men with their backs toward the temple of the LORD and their faces toward the east, and they were worshiping the sun toward the east. (Ezek. 8:16)

Just think of it: In God's holy city, in His holy temple, were His chosen people:

- bowing down before the statue of a false god,
- offering incense to images of creeping things and beasts,
- weeping for Tammuz, the Babylonian nature god, and
- turning their backs toward the temple of the Lord in order to worship the sun toward the east.

The Lord's response to this idolatrous scene is recorded in the final verse in Ezekiel 8:

Therefore I also will act in fury. My eye will not spare nor will I have pity: and though they cry in My ears with a loud voice, I will not hear them. (v. 18)

Herbert Schlossberg's comments are appropriate for both Isaiah's and Ezekiel's days:

In turning away from God, the nation had not fallen into irreligion, but had combined the temple religion with the pagan beliefs and practices of the surrounding peoples. The worship of the God of the Exodus had been defiled by merging it with the worship of idols. *When judgment finally came to the nation, it fell on this syncretistic perversion.* (emphasis mine)[3]

What happened to the people of Israel was the very thing God had so strongly warned them against before they entered the Promised Land:

So it shall be, when the LORD your God brings you into the land of which He swore to your fathers, to Abraham, Isaac, and Jacob, to give you large and beautiful cities which you did not build, houses full of all good things, which you did not fill, hewn-out wells which you did not dig, vineyard and olive trees which you did not plant—when you have eaten and are full—then beware lest you forget the LORD who brought you out of the land of Egypt, from the house of bondage. You shall fear the LORD your God and serve Him, and shall take oaths in His name. You shall not go after other gods, the gods of the peoples who are all around you (for the LORD your God is a jealous God among you), lest the anger of the LORD your God be aroused against you and destroy you from the face of the earth. (Deut. 6:10–15)

As we move toward the end of the twentieth century, even the most optimistic observers are concerned about the spiritual direction of our nation. We also seem to have ignored the warnings of God.

The spiritual decline is so significant that one writer has suggested our approach to evangelism has dramatically changed.

The previous generation of evangelicals were responding to the atheism of that time . . . so they set out to prove that there was an affirmative answer to the question "Is there a God?" But today the question to answer is "Which God?"[4]

This book is about those other gods—the humanistic and occultic influences—that have made inroads into our homes, schools, businesses, and even our churches.

I hope and pray you will read every chapter carefully. Each contains stories of believers and basically moral nonbelievers who have been enticed by a powerful network that used to be called New Age but is now camouflaged in respectability. If you are like those who have heard me preach on this subject, you will be surprised at the level of infiltration these "other gods" have already accomplished in your world.

The last time I heard Francis Schaeffer speak before he died, he left an indelible mark on my life. I cannot tell you the topic upon which he spoke. I remember very little about the speech itself. What I do recall vividly is his spirit of love and concern for the churches and the people of this nation. Knowing there were preachers in his audience, he kept asking, "Where are the tears . . . ?"

Where is the brokenness and compassion for our nation that is forsaking God? Where are the tears?

I hope you will see the tears in this book as you are confronted with the growing seduction of the New spirituality.

1

THE SNARE OF THE SAVAGE WOLVES

WENDY WAS DESPERATE. WHY COULDN'T SHE become pregnant? When she married Bob, her childhood sweetheart, they agreed to wait for three years before they tried to have a baby. Now their fifth anniversary had past, but the nursery was still empty.

No fertility method worked. Wendy thought of little else, and she prayed fervently that next month would bring them good news—only to meet with another disappointment. She became increasingly depressed and felt that she had failed as a wife.

Friends offered her various kinds of advice—some supportive and some useless. One day, Lisa, her best friend, said, "Look . . . I went to this psychic when I was trying to find a job. She told me I would be hired soon and would work in a bank. Well, the next week I got a job at First National. Maybe coincidence, maybe not, but why don't you find out what she'll tell you? What have you got to lose?"

At first Wendy turned down the idea because she thought it was silly, and besides, as a Christian, she knew she shouldn't go. However, Lisa kept pressuring her, so finally she thought, *Why not? I've tried everything else.*

The two women went to an office in a small industrial park containing cellular phone outlets, data survey firms, and other entrepreneurial enterprises. The brass nameplate on the door said, "Personal Consultations." They were greeted by a young receptionist and asked to fill out a simple form that included the reason for the visit and how the client was referred. Harmless enough. They were shown to a room that looked like a doctor's office. An attractive young woman in a conservative suit sat behind the desk and, with a smile, gestured for them to sit down. She asked them if they would like a cup of tea. No crystals, shawls, or garish jewelry here.

Wendy's apprehension began to melt, and she told the psychic about her concerns and fears in a way she had not even confessed to her husband.

"We want a baby, but I'm having trouble getting pregnant. I'm so depressed over this whole thing that I feel sick. I was hoping you might be able to help me," she said tearfully.

After the psychic wrote down Wendy's birthdate and asked her a few questions about her health, she closed her eyes and spoke in a soft, low voice. "I can see that concern about your future family is weighing heavily on you and that it might be interfering with your ability to conceive. You seem to be so terrified by childlessness that you may be communicating this emotion to the entities that might otherwise want to join your family as your children."

Wendy leaned forward, not wanting to lose a word.

"Your fear of losing a child is so spiritually powerful that even if a child chooses your womb, he or she may find it impossible to remain."

She began to speak faster, tilting her head back and looking upward. Wendy seemed transfixed, intent on the psychic's words. "In fact, you have a choice facing you now: You *are* pregnant, but your fear will overwhelm your child, and you will lose it. It will never be born alive."

Wendy choked back a sob as the psychic continued. "However, do not despair. From this tragic experience you will learn to destroy your fear with the divine presence of peace and light, and you will bear other healthy children."

Wendy stumbled out of the office, not wanting to believe the psychic but realizing that the prediction was so unexpected and horrifying she couldn't dismiss it.

The next day her obstetrician confirmed that she was going to have a baby. Instead of the exultation he expected, Wendy began to sob. After hearing her story, the doctor, a Christian, tried to reassure her with both medical and spiritual advice.

"Psychics might trick you into thinking they know the future, but God is the only One who knows for sure," said the doctor while turning the pages in the Bible lying on his desk.

"Here . . . look in Isaiah 8:19–20: 'And when they say to you, "Seek those who are mediums and wizards, who whisper and mutter," should not a people seek their God? Should they seek the dead on behalf of the living? To the law and to the testimony! If they do not speak according to this word, it is because there is no light in them.'

"There are no medical indications that anything will happen to your baby, Wendy. Trust God for your pregnancy and successful childbirth."

Because Wendy was so distraught, the doctor arranged for her to come in once a week for a reassurance checkup, and he gave her his home phone number so she could reach him whenever she needed.

For several weeks the doctor counseled Wendy every time she saw him and assured her that the baby was growing normally and she had nothing to fear. But instead of getting better, she became more emotionally distraught. One week she missed her appointment without any explanation, and the concerned doctor called to find out what was wrong. Wendy's husband answered.

The doctor's voice was concerned. "Wendy missed her appointment yesterday, and I wanted to reschedule."

There was silence on the line for what seemed like an eternity, and then Wendy's husband stammered, "It's no use, Doctor . . . she won't be coming in. She couldn't stand not knowing what was going to happen . . . she was dreading the future. Yesterday she ended it. She had an abortion. When she came home she told me, 'See, the psychic was right.'

This is a true story, relayed to us by Wendy's pastor

"What have you got to lose?" was tragic advice from a friend.

Vast numbers of people inside and outside the church are being caught in subtle satanic traps as they seek answers to life's pain and problems or search for some missing spiritual dimension. They are like innocent animals who fall into a pit disguised with leaves and green grass.

Psychics may display painted signs that say, "Come in," but another far more deadly invitation is capturing the masses in the Western world today. It is the open door that is enticing people of all ages and backgrounds to enter a world of new spiritual experiences, a world that has been altered to meet the needs of this generation. This world is like a movie set with entangled cables and wooden props hiding behind the elaborate facade of a millionaire's empty mansion.

The Shepherd and the Wolves

In 1990, I preached a series of messages on the New Age movement. When these talks were aired on "Turning Point," my radio program, the response was overwhelming. Many in my own congregation came up to me and said, "Dr. Jeremiah, I was involved in some of the practices you described. I had no idea how dangerous they were."

I love to teach the plain message of Scripture, uncovering the rich meanings of the passages so people can take the valuable lessons and truths of God's Word and use them in their own lives. But I am also convinced that we must be aware of the evils and subtle deceptions in our world so that we can apply God's Word defensively.

When the apostle Paul was leaving to go to Jerusalem, he gathered the elders of the Ephesian church and said to them: "I know this, that after my departure savage wolves will come in among you, not sparing the flock. Also from among yourselves men will rise up, speaking perverse things, to draw away the disciples after themselves. Therefore watch, and remember that for three years I did not cease to warn everyone night and day with tears" (Acts 20:29–31).

Every time I read those words I think of the fact that one day, as a pastor, I will give a farewell speech to somebody I have taught, and I hope that I will be able to say with Paul that I have not ceased to teach what the Word of God says, and I have sounded a warning.

In 1990, John Naisbitt wrote in *Megatrends 2000,* "With no membership lists or even a coherent philosophy or dogma, it is more difficult to define or measure the unorganized New Age movement. But in every major U.S. and European city thousands who seek insight and personal growth cluster around a metaphysical bookstore, a spiritual teacher, or an educational center."[1] Since Naisbitt embraces the New Age philosophy, he was not warning; he was reporting.

Only three years after I preached about the New Age, the caution signs went red. A cancer was growing in the American culture that was more invasive than the heresies of the eighties and early nineties. New Age was attempting to hide its occultic roots and gain respectability. Its more prominent followers tried to change their semantics to remove any negativism associated with the name.

New Age spokesman and seminar leader Dick Sutphen made this statement:

> One of the biggest advantages we have as New Agers is once the occult, metaphysical and New Age terminology is removed, we have concepts and techniques that are very acceptable to the general public. So we can change the names and demonstrate the power, and in doing so, we can open the door to millions who normally would not be receptive.[2]

That is what the New Spirituality is all about. Change the names. Demonstrate the power.

My warning has become more urgent. The "savage wolves" are dressed for success.

Out of the Past

When actress Shirley MacLaine danced onto center stage in the 1980s with her book *Out on a Limb,* I thought her descriptions of spirit guides leading into her past lives, out-of-body experiences, trance-channeling, and other occult practices were dangerous views, but I didn't believe she would have a large following among thinking people. *Who would take this other-world mysticism seriously?* I thought.

I was very wrong.

Out on a Limb was on *the New York Times* bestseller list for over fifteen weeks and sold more than two million copies. MacLaine promoted her philosophy before millions of viewers on nationally televised programs and says she received more than forty thousand letters from readers and viewers who wanted to learn more about her reincarnation philosophy. MacLaine's mysticism was embraced by hundreds of thousands who evidently were intrigued by her alternative spirituality.

A conglomerate of Eastern philosophies, spiritual aberrations, and political agendas emerged that was called "a leaderless but powerful network . . . working to bring about radical change in the United States," according to Marilyn Ferguson, an articulate New Age spokesperson.[3]

We have always had fringe movements that march in a different direction from the prevailing Judeo-Christian majority. Most of them have withered with time or failed to gain momentum. Like the stages in our children's growth, I would say, "This, too, will pass." Others said that the New Age philosophy was just a fad, like Hula-Hoops and flower children.

However, I became increasingly aware that ideas once considered "bizarre" were finding their way into our American culture. New Age devotees have turned in their headbands and icons and donned business suits. Their targets are the schools, the media, corporate America, government, healthcare, and our churches. New Age is no longer standing outside the door; it has stepped into the home and invaded mainstream America, just as the Medes and Persians crept into Babylon while Belshazzar was throwing a drunken party (see Dan. 5:1–31).

In 1994, for instance, a little-known author catapulted to fame with his first novel, *The Celestine Prophecy*. This book was on the *New York Times* bestseller list for many weeks. It is a story of an American's adventure in Peru while searching for "the Manuscript," which was said to contain nine insights into life and spirituality. Some critics called it "New Age pop psychology," but its author, James Redfield, wanted to distance himself from that identification.

"[*The Celestine*] *Prophecy* isn't New Age nonsense. The New Age was hilarious," he said, "people wearing little pyramids on their heads, pursuing it in a pretentious way. But wherever there's a counterfeit, there's also the real thing. This book puts into words how to experience spirituality."

Redfield continued, "The world doesn't need another Shirley MacLaine."[4]

However, here's what this bestselling author wrote about his fictional hero's out-of-body experience:

> All I wanted to do was immerse myself in the feeling of being suspended, floating, amid a space that existed in all directions. Rather than having to push myself away from the Earth with my legs as I stood there, resisting the Earth's gravity, I now felt as though I was held up by some inner buoyancy, as though I was filled like a balloon with just enough helium to hover over the ground and barely touch it with my feet.[5]

How strangely similar to Redfield is this passage from New Ager Shirley MacLaine's book *Out on a Limb*:

> Had my spiritual energy separated itself from the physical form? Was I floating *as* my soul? I was consciously aware of my questions as I soared freely above the Earth. I was so conscious of what I felt that in those moments I understood how irrelevant my physical body was.[6]

Redfield denies association with the New Age but espouses the same concepts as Shirley MacLaine did ten years previously. It's like the person who dislikes his name, so he changes it; but he's still the same person.

Without a Life Jacket

We are in the second wave of the New Age and can be caught in the tide if we don't have a life preserver.

At a conference for Christian women, one participant commented on how the spiritual values in *The Celestine Prophecy* were similar to a Christian's search for the meaning of life.

The rationale for her remarks was based upon the fact that Redfield quoted this Scripture:

> And those who have insight will shine brightly like the brightness of the expanse of Heaven, and those who lead the many to righteousness, like the stars forever and ever. But for you, Daniel, conceal these words and seal up the book until the end of time. Many will go back and forth and *knowledge will increase*. (Dan. 12:3–4 emphasis mine)

Many people quote the Bible to make a point, but this passage seemed out of context in Redfield's book.

In his foreword he wrote, "For over half a century now, a new consciousness has been entering the human world, a new awareness that can only be called transcendent, spiritual." Consequently, Redfield might have seen this passage from the prophet Daniel as validating his own beliefs about a new spiritual awareness.

Incidentally, I believe Daniel 12 means knowledge of the end times will increase as we approach the second coming of Christ.

In my 1992 book *The Handwriting on the Wall*, I made this comment:

> There is a time in the future when an understanding of the Book of Daniel will be even greater than it is now. I believe that will be in the time of the end when many are going to be running back and forth, trying to figure out what is happening in their world. Ultimately, they are going to discover answers to their questions in this book [Daniel] we have been studying.[7]

The woman at the Christian conference did not discern the difference between a person's spiritual search involving out-of-body experiences from the one who searches the Scriptures for the truth that saves. The life preservers are available, but the passengers are being directed below deck.

The New Spirituality

In the 1960s the hippie movement wanted a life free of responsibilities and national loyalties. "Make love, not war" was the battle cry. Vietnam separated Americans into doves and hawks, and the deaths of President John Kennedy, Attorney General Robert Kennedy, and Martin Luther King fueled national unrest. There were marches on Washington, burnings and riots on college campuses, and doubts that America could survive the violent decade.

The 1970s saw the flower children beginning to fade and inflation starting to blossom. Even the cost of mailing a first-class letter increased from ten to thirteen cents. We were shocked by the Manson family murders and the kidnapping of heiress Patty Hearst. A Gallup poll showed that 40 percent of U.S. adults attended church services weekly, although mainline churches were beginning to lose members.

Materialism marked the 1980s. Fortunes were made as inflation escalated real estate values. America had a new wave of patriotism and optimism with the crisis of the communist system—and concomitantly of the USSR—becoming increasingly more profound in the mid-eighties, and with the fall of the Berlin Wall in November of 1989. The world seemed to be in overdrive as news events with international implications multiplied faster than snow in Vail, Colorado, or popcorn at a ball game.

The decade of the 1990s has seen the optimism of the past dwindle as the American scene is clouded with violent crime and widespread immorality. Our moral compass is off course, and people are searching for the missing spiritual dimension. Those of the baby boomer generation, now in their thirties and forties, make up close to one out of two households, and many are frightened about the future. They see their children being exposed to more immorality, violence choking their cities, and government eating their dollars. On the other hand, they are open to spiritual concerns—"if they are approached in the right way," says Russell Chandler, author of *Racing Toward 2001*.

Never has there been a time that the prophecy of Daniel about many going "back and forth" while knowledge is increasing seemed more appropriate. Surely more people are trying to figure out what is happening in our world, wondering, *Is God still in charge?*

When a *U.S. News and World Report* poll asked "Do you believe in God or a universal spirit?" 93 percent said yes, and only 5 percent answered no.[8] A "universal spirit" could mean anything from a tree to a toad! "One nation under God" has lost its meaning if there are many gods.

A Princeton University sociologist, Robert Wuthnow, said, "We are becoming less theologically and institutionally grounded and more inclined toward making up our own faiths as we go along."[9]

The New Spirituality is tolerant of all the religions of the world, even those that are diametrically opposed to one another. Its deception comes when no line is drawn between right and wrong. Someone may proclaim to be a Christian and yet embrace an incompatible non-Christian pluralism, like M. Scott Peck, author of the bestselling book *The Road Less Traveled,* who frequently uses Christian terminology and considers himself a convert to Christianity and yet who inconsistently proclaims in the sequel, *Further Along the Road Less Traveled:*

> God, unlike some organized religions, does not discriminate. As long as you reach out to Her, She will go the better part of the way to meet you. There are an infinite number of roads to reach God. People can come to God through alcoholism, they can come to God through Zen Buddhism, as I did, and they can come to God through the multiple "New Thought" Christian churches even though they are distinctly heretical. For all I know, they can come to God through Shirley MacLaine. People are at various stages of readiness, and when they're ready, virtually anything can speak to them.[10]

Major Religious World Systems

To place the New Spirituality in perspective, we should categorize the four major religious world systems. They basically consist of words that have the word *theism* in them (from *theos*, which means god).

The dictionary definition of religion is "an organized system of beliefs and rituals centering on a supernatural being or beings," or "a belief upheld or pursued with zeal and devotion."[11]

One religious system is *monotheism*, which is made up of two words: *mono*, or one, and *theism*, meaning god. A monotheist is somebody who believes there is one God in the universe and that He exists outside of the universe He created. There are three major world religions whose basic tenet is monotheistic.

First, there is *Christianity*, which is unique among major world faiths for teaching that one eternal, personal, loving, and infinite God exists in three persons, Father, Son, and Holy Spirit.

Judaism is also monotheistic: "Hear, O Israel: The LORD our God, the LORD is one!" (Deut. 6:4). This statement, known as the *Shema*, epitomizes the faith of the Jews. Contemporary Judaism rejects the Trinity and the deity of Jesus Christ.

It may come as a surprise that *Islam* is also monotheistic; followers believe in one god, although it is not the true God. If you have ever heard a Muslim prayer, it is addressed to one god because one of the five pillars of Islam is "There is no God but the one God, and Mohammed is His prophet."

Islam rejects the doctrine of the Trinity and considers Jesus to be one of the great prophets. Allah differs from the Jewish and Christian concept of God because he is morally capricious; he declares what is good or evil, and his declaration makes it true. The Muslim has no assurance of what it takes to please Allah and be welcomed into eternal paradise.

The second world-view is *atheism*. When you put the letter *a* in front of the word, it takes away the content of the word it prefixes. Atheism means "no god." Atheists have no belief in God, and most of them believe that the material universe began with the Big Bang; they refuse to speculate on whether anything existed before that time, or they say, "it just happened." *Secular humanists* are atheistic; they believe that the very idea of God is irrelevant and irrational.

Agnostics do not fall in the same category as atheists because they don't know whether any deity exists. Witches, for instance, would be considered agnostic because they practice rituals and use terminology of polytheism and pantheism, but they admit that they do not know if any "divine essence" exists. One of the girls who answers the phone at our radio ministry was startled to have a male caller identify himself as a warlock. She wasn't sure what that meant until he explained he was a male witch. For twenty minutes he gave her a lecture on the fact that there were good witches and bad witches, and that I was bigoted in my denunciation of all witchcraft.

"Listen, I want you to know that Dr. Jeremiah doesn't know what he's talking about," he said. "Not all witches are bad, and not all witches serve the devil. Most of us don't believe in either God or the devil."

The poor girl was quite upset about the whole conversation, but when she reported it to me the next morning I was elated.

"I'm grateful for one thing," I said. "The witch who was listening heard an accurate view of witchcraft from the Scriptures."

The third category of major world religions is called *polytheism*. The prefix *poly* means many or more than one, so polytheists are those who believe there are many gods. They believe that the gods don't necessarily have eternal existence but that people who were not gods become gods. According to a polytheist, there are many gods that are in operation.

Greek and Roman mythology have many kinds of gods: Zeus, Venus, Apollos, etc. People in South America and Africa who practice *voodoo* are polytheists. *Mormonism* is polytheistic because Mormons believe that God was once a man and that man can become God. If you read the Mormon literature, you will find that to be very carefully stated in what they write about themselves.[12]

The fourth major religious belief is more challenging to understand. Within its scope of beliefs is the term *pantheism*. *Pan* means all, so a pantheist believes that everything is god. I am god. You are god. Your pet dog is god. Everything is god.

Actually a pantheist is a god with amnesia. He needs to recover his godhead, and if he could just remember that he is god, he'll be okay. His salvation comes from realizing his own divinity, sometimes called self-realization or Christ-consciousness.

Buddhism and *New Ageism* are pantheistic, as is *Hinduism* and its sects, such as *Hare Krishnas*, even though they embrace polytheism as well. They consider all of underlying reality to be divine, with particular divine manifestations as gods and goddesses.

The New Age movement is both pantheistic and polytheistic. However, it is now being repackaged to present a more attractive product. This is not a result of organized research and development. No group of men or women cloistered in a closed room decided to start a counterculture spiritual revolution. I do not believe in a conspiracy theory, for that implies a tightly organized movement that can be easily identified and exposed. Movements based upon loose affiliation are harder to classify and more elusive to describe.

The New Spirituality has replaced New Age in the supermarket of beliefs, and millions are buying its poisonous products.

Undercurrent of the New Spirituality

If you had a high fever, just taking aspirin wouldn't unearth the source of the infection. The New Spirituality contains certain basic beliefs that are contagious. When we apply a stethoscope to the New Spirituality we can hear the New Age heartbeat. It's the same disorder, but now instead of simply being visible it has spread through the entire American body.

The first fundamental precept is belief in the *universality of God*. This is a pantheistic view that is described by a character in J. D. Salinger's short story *Teddy*. A spiritually precocious youngster recalls watching his little sister drink her milk. He says, "All of a sudden I saw that she was God. And the milk was God. All she was doing was pouring God into God."[13]

According to this view, there is no real distinction between humankind and nature; matter, time, and space are unreal myths that must be eliminated. There is no end goal of life in pantheism.

A person must simply move through countless illusory incarnations until he or she is absorbed into the great "One" like a drop of water falling into the ocean.

Instead of an omnipotent God, there is the cosmic force of the universe. This world-view says that God is in everything, so whatever exists, whether it is a person, a pig, or a pickle, is part of God.

The problem with this belief is that God's Word teaches that all is *not* God. God stands outside of the creation; Ecclesiastes 5:2 says God is in His heaven and you are on the earth. The Bible presents God as an independent person who communicates, plans, demonstrates emotion, and has the ability to choose. As the creator, God is distinct from His creation. It is a terrible travesty of truth to say all is God and God is all.

The second infectious precept of the New or Alternative Spirituality is that *there is no difference between good and bad.* If everything is God, then what is bad is God and what is good is God, and there really isn't any distinction. The universe, according to this view, is amoral.

If you talk with a person who has accepted these views, he or she might say, "You're a Christian? That's great. Hey, whatever. Just do your thing; we're all a part of the universe. I'm just my own person, but you do whatever you want. Whatever works for you is fine."

The Bible teaches there is right and wrong and that God has set standards for us to follow. The New Spirituality teaches that there can be no sin against God if everyone is a part of God, but the Bible clearly says that man's problem is disobedience against his personal God. Until we understand that problem, we can never find what we are looking for in our own lives.

A third factor in this disease is belief in the *unity of the cosmos,* which teaches that all reality, including God, humankind, the created universe, earth, time, space, and energy, are all connected in divine consciousness. As one circles the eternal wheel of existence, one regains the divine conscious and the realization that he or she—and all of existence—is God.

A news report from a conference in New Mexico said that a woman stood transfixed, her eyes closed, her hands grasping the leaves of a tree. She said she was getting nourishment from

Mother Nature by trying to feel one with the tree. She was searching for a connection with some "cosmic consciousness."

The Bible teaches that we are individuals even before we are born. We are distinct, unique beings who one day will stand before God and give an account of what we have done and how we have lived. We won't be able to hide behind any tree, cosmic or otherwise.

Fourth, those who accept this Alternative Spirituality also believe in the *finality of experience:* You validate what you believe according to your experience—"I know this is real because it happened to me."

"How do you know God?" is a question people have asked from the beginning of human history. The Old Testament describes how Job, almost four thousand years ago, struggled with his own understanding of God. Today that same struggle continues. Many people believe that God reveals Himself through some mystical experience. I heard of one person who said, "I saw a vision of God in the clouds. It was the image of a man reaching out to me with such a look of love that I couldn't resist stretching out my hands to touch him. Everyone comes to God in a different way. For me, it was that day in the Red Rock Canyon of Arizona when God came to me. It was truly a 'born again' experience."

The Bible says there is only one way a person can be saved, and that is through Jesus Christ (Acts 4:12). When there is no body of truth, no absolutes, when everything is right and everything is wrong at the same time, anyone can say anything and his or her own subjective experiences become the needed validation.

"But I saw a UFO with my own eyes."

"I spoke with my dead husband. He was standing by the door."

"I went to heaven and met Jesus but returned to earth."

It is difficult to talk to people who have had a "spiritual" experience until you can show them that unless that experience is based upon biblical truth it is unreliable.

The New Spirituality gives us carte blanche in our behavior. There is no right or wrong; it's everyone's personal experience that is the final judge.

I have a non-Christian friend I meet with regularly. He comes to church, hears me preach, and knows I believe in God. But that's not enough for him. He is trying to understand rationally who Jesus Christ was as a historic person so he can come to faith. My experience isn't going to help this man because someone else can come in and say, "Let me tell you about *my* experience." Then it's that person's experience versus my experience, and there is nothing to establish who is right.

Brian O'Leary was a NASA scientist-astronaut during the Apollo program. He has a Ph.D. in astronomy from the University of California at Berkeley and has served on the faculties of Cornell University, Cal Tech, and Princeton. He said:

> In 1979, when I was a physics faculty member at Princeton University, I had a powerful psychic experience in which I was able to accurately describe the characteristics of a total stranger. . . . Subsequent experiences, ranging from a healing to a near-death experience, as well as research visits to laboratories with gifted people worldwide, gradually convinced me we are in for big changes as the new millennium approaches.[14]

Someone with the prestigious background of an astronaut can influence many with his experience. However, experience is not the criterion for a Christian. The Bible tells us that Satan leads the whole world astray and that he masquerades as an angel of light. He is adept at getting people to believe in things that are not true.

Fifth, New Spirituality is the belief in the necessity of *higher consciousness*. According to this view, when you are walking around in a sound body and sound mind you can't be religious; you must get out of your body, out of your mind, so that you can ascend to the next level, to your higher consciousness. With trances, mediums, and spirit guides, you can attain your higher consciousness and be absorbed into the universe. This is the real meaning in life.

Sixth, New Spirituality calls for the *intercession of higher spirits*. Psychics and mediums have been with us since King Saul disguised himself and slipped into Endor to ask a woman who was a medium to conduct a seance for him. Today, we can view a medium on television in our own living rooms.

Who would have thought a few years ago that we would see major ads for psychics on TV? We only need to turn the channel to see movie stars inviting us to call a 900 number where we can be in touch with someone who can help us with all our problems. Today, if you are eighteen years of age or older, for just $3.25 a minute, the commercial says, you may have an online consultation with your very own psychic.

A psychic claims to have special knowledge of events (past, present, or future) and people. He or she gets the knowledge through the "divine vibrations" of an article of clothing, by means of "angelic" visitations, through analysis of astrological charts, or a variety of other means.

On a program called *Your Lucky Stars,* a group of very attractive, well-dressed women invited members of the audience to consult them. The announcer said, "These women, with their incredible God-given ability, can give you information on love, money, relationships, job opportunities, or business decisions."

Do psychics have "God-given ability," as the distinguished host claimed? The Bible says, "The Spirit clearly says that in the latter times some will abandon the faith and will follow deceiving spirits and things taught by demons" (1 Tim. 4:1).

When you open your mind to the influence of demons, you have allowed Satan to get a foot in the door of your life. Some will be drawn into the demon world because they succumbed to an ad on television. It is chocolate-coated candy with a poisonous center.

Filling the Emptiness

Marxism is gone or in total disarray. Capitalism appears helpless before Third World hunger. Materialism has been weighed in the balance and found wanting. In fact, leisure time is replacing money as the number one desire. In too many places the Christian church possesses a passionless "head knowledge" about God. The house has been swept clean, and people are looking for new answers. The second wave of the New Age has gained a respectable foothold in places we would never have believed it could invade.

As we shall see, it has infiltrated ministerial associations, our educational system, medical offices, and even has taken up residence in the White House. It is the subject of countless talk shows, and no one is laughing at the new Eastern way of looking at things anymore.

So I urge you not to believe the New Age movement is passé. If you can open your eyes to it, you can build a wall of fire around yourself to keep it from ever touching your life.

While America still has the dominant role in international leadership, it is a leadership that is post-Christian. Humanistic spirituality is filling the void.

When I began to teach on the "Second Wave of the New Age," I received a rather salty letter from a lady who said, "When are you going to quit talking about all this New Age and New Spirituality stuff and go back to preaching the Bible?"

I answered the dear lady that my greatest joy is preaching from the Bible. Scripture is full of warnings. I believe the New Spirituality is the greatest threat to the Christian world-view today. It is subtle and insidious, ready to catch us unaware. My warning is not from an academic viewpoint; it is with the passion of the apostle Paul when he said, "I did not cease to warn everyone night and day . . . with tears."

How did a peril of such cancerous proportion assault our present age? Where did it all begin? That's the question we will strive to answer

2

INVASION
FROM THE EAST

THREE HANDSOME YOUNG MONKS IN scarlet-and-gold robes bent over a table, filling in an elaborate design with patterns of colored sand. They were creating their Wheel of Compassion mandala, a sacred sand painting as exquisite as fine embroidery and an integral part of Buddhist teaching rituals.

Starting at the center of a circle, they drew a "lotus flower with eight petals—homes of the deities of compassion." Nearby were some youngsters who had been following the monks' instructions and were creating their own mandalas. In the center they drew a peace symbol.

Is this in Calcutta or Bombay? No, guess again. It happened in Watts, the inner city of Los Angeles, and was sponsored by the New York-based Samaya Foundation, whose mission it is to bring Tibetan culture to Westerners.

On the last day of the course, which was called "Healing the Causes of Violence through Art," the monks and their proteges, following Tibetan ritual, swept their mandalas into a sacred urn that was to be emptied into the sea.

This sounds like an innocent enough program, except that the mission of the ceremony was that "the mandalas have fulfilled their purposes. The deities will be asked to return to their celestial abodes. The consecrated sand will purify the water; the water will evaporate into the clouds and the cleansing rain will fall."[1]

A few months later, in another city, we encounter a similar happening.

> For a few minutes an audience was transported to a lost kingdom: a place where prayer flags snap in a cold wind, harsh mountain sunlight reflects off temple rooftops and a procession of monks in red robes winds down a hillside like a river of blood.
>
> Sitting cross-legged on a gym floor singing traditional Buddhist prayers, Tibetan monks evoked this lost world with only the tones of their voices.

This is the common practice in Tibet, but this was not Tibet; this was San Diego, California, and the event occurred at the Mesa College gym.

> The size and diversity of the crowds attending the week of events reflect the growing popularity of Tibetan-style Buddhism in the United States, and Buddhism in general.[2]

These stories, reported in the *Los Angeles Times* and the *San Diego Union-Tribune*, are other indications of how Eastern mysticism has infiltrated America.

Does this seem dangerous? Once we understand how its influence has caused millions of people to take a spiritual journey leading to a dead end, we will realize just how dangerous it is to us individually and to our society.

Before Buddha, There Was Hinduism

A monk by the name of Siddhartha Gautama wandered through India twenty-five hundred years ago and was known as Buddha, or "the Enlightened One." As a philosophy, Buddhism teaches reincarnation and karma, just as Hinduism does. The two religions differ, however, since Hinduism is clearly religious pantheism while Buddhism embraces a nonreligious monism, which is closer to atheism than anything else.

Today the way of the Buddha has more than 309 million followers worldwide, with 554,000 in North America, and Hinduism has 719 million worldwide, with 1.26 million in North America.[3]

Hinduism predates Buddhism by at least a thousand years and is one of the oldest world belief systems and the most baffling. It is unorganized, has no national church system, and embraces many contradictory beliefs, meaning different things to its vast number of devotees.

Hinduism traces its source to sacred scriptures called "the *Vedas*" (which means knowledge). This assortment of books is considered to be divinely inspired by Hindu gods and interpreted by ancient Hindu seers. This collection of religious literature bears the imprint of spiritistic influences.

Hinduism may be defined as the religious beliefs and practices common to India. One writer said that Hinduism is noted as being the only one of the major beliefs that cannot be defined.[4] Another described it as a religion based on mythology because it has neither a founder (as do Buddhism, Islam, and Christianity) nor a fixed canon.[5]

But in spite of its diversity, Hinduism in general does reveal a number of common themes. Some of these include pantheism (the belief that all is God and God is all), polytheism (a belief in many lesser gods), and a reliance upon occultic ritual and practices.[6]

If you've ever pulled a thread from something you were wearing and had an entire seam unravel, you'll understand a little of the influence of Hinduism. If we grab some of its beliefs and give them a pull, a jumble of religious movements fall out.

All religions have the right to build their churches, synagogues, and temples, but the Hindu influence is undermining the Judeo-Christian roots of American culture. Millions of Americans have taken up Hindu practices such as yoga, meditation, developing altered states of consciousness, seeking Hindu "enlightenment," and various occultic practices.[7]

If Hinduism is packaged as love and light, a religion of tolerance and nonviolence, but is, in fact, something else, then we need to understand some of its beliefs and be able to recognize its dangers.

Eastern Roots

There were no boatloads of Hindu refugees landing at Ellis Island nor Indian intellectuals seeking asylum to preach their gospel. Americans began to hear of Hinduism more than 150 years ago when Christian missionaries went to India and came back with reports about social evils such as idolatry and the caste system, which were the result of Hinduism.

In the middle of the last century, an unschooled mystic began to make a name for himself in India with his new theology. Hindu priest Ramakrishna had spiritual experiences that led him to experiment with other sects of Hinduism and other religions, and he began to preach the unity of all religions. Various religious doctrines, he said, were nothing more than human opinions—in the modern vernacular, "all paths lead to God." Ramakrishna's point was that religion does not really deal with doctrines or historical accuracy; it is *experience* that counts.

Falling under the influence of Ramakrishna was an English-educated aristocrat. At first, he was a critic of the uneducated mystic and went to the temple grounds to argue with him. However, the story goes that the young man, Vivekananda, was touched one day by the Ramakrishna's foot and immediately fell into a trance in which he saw the things around him merging together into one unified reality. From that time on, he became a disciple of Ramakrishna.

In many ways, Vivekananda was unlike his mentor. He was troubled by India's grinding poverty and social backwardness but believed that the Western nations needed India for its spiritual legacy. He proposed a renewal of spiritual life in Europe and America, guided by Hinduism.[8]

One hundred years ago, Vivekananda appeared at the World Parliament of Religions, which met in Chicago. One day he addressed all the delegates, and the *Chicago Tribune* printed parts of his talk in which he admonished the delegates for their "imperialist" attitudes toward Eastern religions. He accused the Christians of being patronizing and intolerant.

He must have made quite an impression, even though the audience was shocked. He opened the door for what was called a "creative synthesis of traditional Hindu ideas and modern scientific and democratic thought."[9]

The roots were beginning to be established. Vivekananda's legacy to the Western world was the founding of the Vedanta Society (a system of Hindu philosophy based on the *Vedas*), which now maintains branches in major cities of the United States and Western Europe.

Following this came an array of famous names who added their luster to modern Vedanta. Rabindranath Tagore, who lived until 1941, was its poet, philosopher, and social reformer, and Mahatma Gandhi was its most prominent politician and a leader in India's struggle for independence.

The roots began to grow stronger when a diminutive, giggling Hindu, Guru Maharishi Mahesh Yogi, appeared in the 1960s and 70s to bring a message of utopia to America—a virtual heaven on earth. It was called Transcendental Meditation, or TM.

Transcendental Meditation is a somewhat simplified yoga technique designed to alter one's consciousness. John Weldon, a Christian who has a broad understanding of the influence of Eastern thought and cultic practices, was a follower of TM at one time. In his book *The Transcendental Explosion,* written with Zola Levitt, Weldon describes an initiation ceremony where the beginner receives his secret mantra, the mysterious sound he will use to meditate. "From then on the new devotee is to meditate twice daily for fifteen or twenty minutes each time, meditating solely on the mantra. This process is supposed to take the mind though increasingly subtle levels of thought down to 'the field of pure creative intelligence,' or 'absolute bliss consciousness.' The ultimate goal is to take one to the 'source of all thought,' or 'pure creative intelligence.'"[10]

Weldon explains that "TM stems from a tradition of occultism, Hinduism, astrology, spiritism and a variety of occult practices that are commonplace in India today."[11]

TM started a movement that swept the United States. Off-shoot organizations sprang up, with such diverse organizations as the Pentagon and AT&T promoting the "benefits" of its practices. Well-known persons such as Joe Namath, Stevie Wonder, Merv Griffin, Clint Eastwood, Peggy Lee, and other celebrities were touted as TM devotees by the Maharishi in his powerful media outreach. He was on a roll![12]

The Maharishi himself hasn't been in the United States for many years but resides in Holland, according to a conversation we had with one of his spokesmen in the Pacific Palisades, California, headquarters. However, the Maharishi International University is thriving in Iowa where there is a whole meditative community, with education provided from preschool through college. The original TM explosion has left its fallout throughout America. When we inquired about TM from the Spiritual Counterfeits Project, a very effective research source on religious movements and cults, one of the researchers said, "The ideas from TM are incorporated into the mainstream today." TM followers have their own political party (the Beach Boys push it in their concerts) and have qualified for the ballot in several states. They also promote anticrime programs in high-crime areas such as Washington, D.C., where they combine social-action programs with meditation.

Not only TM, but many other modern philosophies are based upon Hindu beliefs, which, at first glance, sometimes "sound just like" Christianity. The popular New Age "bible," *A Course in Miracles*, was dictated by an "inner voice" that was Jesus Himself, according to psychologist Helen Schucman, the channel for these amazing "revelations." Choosing biblical terminology to convey its message, the *Course* attempts to camouflage its religious philosophy, which is based on Hindu concepts. Later in this book, our chapter on "Spirit Guides on the Bookshelves" will show how the *Course* has made an impact on bestselling books in the "spiritual" genre.

Listing the fallouts from Hindu thought is like writing a cookbook on the 101 ways to cook vegetables. They may have a different flavor, a different appearance, but they're all grown in the same native soil.

In *The Facts on Hinduism in America*, John Ankerberg and John Weldon list some of the modern religious cults and sects that have been influenced by Hinduism in varying degrees.

Werner Erhard, founder of est and the Forum seminars, was influenced through Swami Muktanda, one of Erhard's principal gurus. Other systems such as Theosophy, Science of Mind, Divine Science, and Unity School of Christianity derive some of their philosophies from Hinduism. The occultic religion of Eckankar is an outgrowth from a Hindu sect known as Radhasoami, and Scientology, with its many centers throughout the world, has been swayed by Hinduism.[13]

Hindu thought patterns and basic Christian beliefs are as diametrically opposed as fire and water. One or the other must dominate.

Who Is God?

Hinduism in America teaches that God is an impersonal divine essence called Brahman. It teaches that everything is God or part of God. This, of course, is pantheism.

In *Teachings of Swami Vivekananda*, we are told that Brahman (God) does not know anything! He is described this way:

> . . . an impersonal omnipresent being who cannot be called a knowing being. . . . He cannot be called a thinking being, because that is a process of the weak only. He cannot be called a reasoning being, because reasoning is a sign of weakness. He cannot be called a creating being, because none creates except in bondage.[14]

Remember, Vivekananda is the same man who brought his vision of spiritual renewal to America more than a hundred years ago. This god of Hinduism he introduced in America is pantheistic, impersonal, unknowing, and unknowable; this god cannot show love because love is a personal attribute.

C. S. Lewis said, "Pantheism is a creed not so much false as hopelessly behind the times. Once, before creation, it would have been true to say that everything was God. But God created: He caused things to be other than Himself that, being distinct, they might learn to love Him, and achieve union instead of mere sameness."[15]

Our God is loving and holy, and we can know Him personally through Jesus Christ. God's love was demonstrated at the cross, where in one act of unparalleled sacrifice, He took all our sins upon Himself and was judged in our place.

In Hinduism, however, such ideas as a personal, loving God are rejected as spiritual ignorance.

Who Is Jesus?

The Hindu gurus typically redefine Jesus after their own likeness. He becomes a teacher of Hinduism, a guru of the past who has been greatly misunderstood by Christians. Indian guru Bhagwan Shree Rajneesh taught:

> To tell you the truth, Jesus is a mental case. . . . He is a fanatic. He carries the same kind of mind as Adolf Hitler. He is a fascist. He thinks that only those who follow him will be saved. . . . And the fools are still believing that they will be saved if they follow Jesus.[16]

Jesus of Nazareth is not, according to Eastern belief, the Son of God, the Lord and Savior of the cosmos; He is merely one of many manifestations of God. The only Jesus the gurus recognize is a Hindu Jesus. They reject who Jesus Christ is when they deny His deity.

Jesus never taught that He was a guru; He said He was the Jewish Messiah and that He was God: "I and My Father are one" (John 10:30). In His life and teachings, we find that He is not only sane and rational, but He said, "I am the way, the truth, and the life. No one comes to the Father except through Me" (John 14:6). He proved that through His works and, most of all, through His own resurrection.

The apostle Paul was counteracting false teaching in the city of Colosse when he wrote to his friends there and accurately described who Christ was and is: "He is the image of the invisible God, the firstborn over all creation. For by Him all things were created that are in heaven and that are on earth, visible and invisible, whether thrones or dominions or principalities or powers. All things were created through Him and for Him. And He is before all things, and in Him all things consist" (Col. 1:15–17).

Who Is Man?

Man and God are one, according to Hinduism. God is within man, and every man is God. Guru Sai Baba said, "You are the God of this universe. You are not a man, you are God."[17]

A typical yoga meditation, which is intended to help the disciple realize that he is God, is repeated by Swami Vishnudevanada:

> I am the light of lights; I am the sun; I am the real, real sun. . . . In me the whole world moves and has its being. . . . I existed before the world began. . . . I permeate and pervade every atom. . . . Oh, how beautiful I am. . . . I am the whole universe . . . everything is in me.[18]

One of the leading popularizers of the New Age movement, Shirley MacLaine, explains in her book *Dancing in the Light* that she takes five minutes every day reminding herself that she is God. She says her daily affirmations make her feel good.

> Affirmations are spoken resolutions which, when used properly, align the physical, mental, and spiritual energies. The ancient Hindu vedas claimed that the spoken words *I am*, or *Aum* in Hindu, set up a vibrational frequency in the body and mind which align the individual with his or her higher self and thus with the God-source. You can use *I am God* or *I am that I am* as Christ often did, or you can extend the affirmation to fit your own needs.[19]

If we have examined the beauty of a flower, the majesty of the mountains, if we have looked at the galaxy of stars on a cloudless night, if we have ever touched a baby's finger or felt rain on our face, how can we think *we* are God?

The Bible says,

> Because your heart is lifted up,
> And you say, "I am a god,
> I sit in the seat of gods,

In the midst of the seas,"
Yet you are a man, and not a god,
Though you set your heart as the heart of a god.
(Ezek. 28:2)

The Bible says we are God's creation, and we must look to our Creator for salvation. It teaches that men and women are sinful and require redemption (forgiveness of sins). If any person's sins are not forgiven in this life, he or she will pay the penalty, after death, of eternal separation from God.

Hinduism says we are divine and salvation is a process that may take millions of lifetimes to work out our "karma" (spiritual imperfections) until we finally merge back into Brahman.

What in the World Is the World?

Hinduism teaches that the world in which we live is ultimately an illusion, a dream of an impersonal Brahman who exists "in" or "underneath" the material creation and is indifferent to what goes on in the world. As far as Hinduism is concerned, Brahman is not the creator, but a mere observer of all events.

The biblical view is that "In the beginning God created the heavens and earth" (Gen. 1:1) and that God is personal, loving, and holy. The Bible clearly teaches that God loves us and that His love was demonstrated when He took on human nature in the person of Jesus Christ. In one act of unparalleled self-denial, He bore all the world's sins upon Himself and was judged in our place. He did this because of His great love for us and His desire that no one should perish (see 2 Pet. 3:9).

The "wisdom from the East" has resulted in a carnage of lives in India. Caryl Matriciana, author of *Gods of the New Age*, tells of her return to the land of her birth and the horror of what she saw in a country where animals are revered and humans are expendable.

Oh, the streets of Calcutta! Pitiful shacks made up of sack-cloth, rags, and sticks engulfed the sidewalks and spilled onto the streets. When our cab stopped for a moment at a traffic light, I was able to peek into the dark interiors of these "homes." I was still horrified, after all these years, to see the number of people living inside.

Sisters and brothers curled against each other like young gerbils in a cage. I remember one pathetically skinny child in tattered rags with cow-dung matted in her hair. She was attempting to soothe another wailing tot. She cuddled and caressed him with smiles and giggles on her sweet sad face.

How could the Western spiritual seekers I had spoken to in England, Europe, and America miss all this tragedy? How could they bypass it to focus on the "wisdom and love of the East"? Couldn't they see that it was the very aloofness and madness of India's religion that resulted in such obvious agony and apathy?[20]

India is the seventh largest landmass in the world and has a population of seven hundred million people. In spite of its size and natural resources, India rates as one of the world's poorest nations. Hinduism has brought about a nation where man is degraded, and yet this is a religion with thought patterns that millions of Americans are embracing.

Out of India

Samuel Nandakumar was a Hindu, raised in an upper-middle-class family in India. His father was a newspaper editor and a temple priest and had come from a long line of priests who had served in the Hindu temple. As a young boy, Nanda knew all the ritual and ceremony connected with his religion.

He majored in chemistry at the University of Madras and regularly made "pujas" (Hindu prayer rituals) to the god and goddess images. He said he was proud that he lived a "good" life, and he never wanted to harm another person. In his final year at college, he began to experience fear, frustration, and panic that was so intense he thought he would have a nervous breakdown. He noticed, however, that one of his friends who had many severe problems had a peace about him that was puzzling. Finally, Nanda asked his friend, "Prakash, here I am, wondering about my sanity, and yet you, who face the same grueling tests as I do, are happy and at ease. How can this be?"

Prakash, who was working with Youth for Christ, told him about a Man sent from God, Jesus Christ, who could bring him peace. "You see, Nanda, according to Hindu tradition, you have done all the right things. But none of them—no penance, no pujas, no washing in the 'holy' River Ganges—can bring you peace inside. These are only external acts."

"Then what can I do?" Nanda asked. "How can I get what you have?"

"Only by believing with your heart that Jesus died for you," Prakash explained. "When Christ suffered on the cross, He took all of your sins upon Himself so that you could be forgiven and have peace with God."

Nanda told us, "I simply knew with my mind and heart that Prakash was telling me the truth." He asked Jesus Christ to come into his heart, and as he continued studying for exams, a soft calm replaced his jagged fears.

When he told his family, they thought he had gone so far astray that they issued an ultimatum to denounce his new faith or leave. Nanda finished college and went to Calcutta, where he fell in love with and married a Christian pastor's daughter. He stayed in that city and taught school for fifteen years. Today he heads a large international ministry in San Jose, California, and has an urgency to reach Hindus for Christ.

When we asked Dr. Nandakumar why so many Westerners are drawn to Eastern practices and thought, he said, "Because it's so complicated."

I admit his answer puzzled me until he explained his premise. "Western intellectuals find that the philosophy and practice of Hinduism is very challenging," he said. "They want the stimulus of discovery, something that stretches their minds. Once they become 'enlightened' they can pass on their beliefs and discoveries to their disciples. Every cult has its roots in Hinduism."

The more we research and study, the more truth we see in Nanda's observation.

Palaniswami, the editor of *Hinduism Today,* wrote an "Open Letter to Evangelicals" in January 1991. In it he said,

"Hinduism will have a surprisingly sophisticated network around the globe in another twenty years."

I do not believe we have to wait twenty years for Palaniswami's predictions to come true. We are witnessing the tremendous surge of Hindu beliefs and practices today.

Christians need to speak "the truth in love" (Eph. 4:15) to the followers of the New Spirituality. We must be equipped to defend the claims of the Christian faith to those who may never have heard its message.

The spiritual seeker is not looking for criticism but for love and acceptance. Hinduism and its influence lose their effectiveness where Christ is preached and the church is alive and well.

You may not accept Hindu beliefs or chant your own mantra, but the siren song of the New Spirituality may be creeping into your home when you thought the doors were locked. Will you recognize its stealthy steps?

3

MANY HAPPY (?) RETURNS

ONE SUNDAY NIGHT IN 1994, people in living rooms across the country settled on their couches with popcorn and drinks to watch one of television's better programs, *The Hallmark Hall of Fame.* On this evening, the venerable married actors Hume Cronyn and Jessica Tandy were starring in a poignant drama. The story was about how one man, played by Hume Cronyn, struggled with his loneliness after the death of his beloved wife.

At a low point in his grief, a little white dog appears at the man's back door, whining for attention. Cronyn reluctantly befriends the animal, finally becoming very devoted to it. One day, his deceased wife (played by Jessica Tandy) comes to him in a vision and assures him that she will not leave him alone but will be with him on earth as long as he lives. In a typical movie portrayal of humans who appear after death, she fades away into a mist; the little white dog appears in her place.

The day after this program, several Christians were commenting on it and one woman remarked, "That was one of the most tender love stories I've ever seen. Wasn't it beautiful the way she communicated with him after she died?"

That "tender love story" was a message about transmigration, pure and simple. It was not overtly evil or bizarre, but the meaning was clear: You and I can return. We may come back

41

many times in many forms. In other words, we may literally have many returns, happy or unhappy.

Many Christians tend to live in a little cocoon, an envelope of safety where they attempt to shut out the reality of the world. They may be inclined to say, "All that stuff about reincarnation is going on, I know, but it's not around here."

Have you seen the movies or videos in your town? *Heaven Can Wait, Heart and Souls, A Guy Named Joe, Dead Again.* Have you watched television lately? Barbara Walters interviewed a woman on *20/20* who was certain she had lived two lives. Ask your neighbors and they might say, "I just have this feeling I lived during the Civil War." Reincarnation is alive (more than once). It has been the subject of jokes for most of the years since I was growing up. For instance: The fundamental question of life for most people has been, "Who am I?" For the reincarnationist, the question is "Who was I?" These people don't have "come as you are" parties; they have "come as you were" parties

Believe me, it isn't a joke today.

Just a short distance from my church and home in Southern California is an organization called Unarius Academy of Science. Its objective, according to its own statements, is "to help the individual progress in his evolution." The Unarius curriculum is designed to lift the consciousness of the individual through courses in past-life therapy.

Ruth Norman, the founder of Unarius, is said to have had many lives: king, queen, artist, scientist, priest, and poet. She also was supposedly the spiritual mentor to Napoleon and also to Mary of Bethany, "the Master's beloved and betrothed, who was the 13th disciple, continued the teachings of Jesus and authored the Book of Revelations."[1]

How unusual. I didn't know Mary of Bethany was the author of the book of Revelation! According to my Bible, the first verse says, "The Revelation of Jesus Christ, which God gave Him to show His servants—things which must shortly take place. And He sent and signified it by His angel to His servant John" (Rev. 1:1).

The Unarius Academy of Science claims to have pioneered the teaching of past-life therapy and states that we can apply the principles of "reincarnation physics" to our lives and thereby step up our progressive evolution in this "New Age of Spiritual Renaissance"! One of the academy's books tells the story of a young man who documented his previous life as Isoroku Yamamoto, commander of the Japanese navy in World War II. The author "recognized his karma and is now functioning with a greater degree of mental clarity, due to his recognition of the distortion of his consciousness from the past!"[2]

Hold on to your space helmets; we haven't arrived yet. The founder of Unarius Academy stated, "The landing of extra-terrestrials from other planets will signal the real beginning of the New Age of Spiritual Renaissance."

We can't draw the blankets over our heads when this exists next door.

Have You Been Here Before?

As we investigated the school that teaches about past-life memories and reincarnation, the claims seemed outlandish. Uriel, nee Ruth Norman, has been in mental contact with thirty-two other worlds within our galaxy. The amazing prophecy she gives is that in the year 2001, when the last remaining barrier of space will be overcome, Planet Earth will become the thirty-third member of the Interplanetary Confederation. At that time, thirty-three spaceships from other planets will arrive on earth, the music will begin, and thirty-three doves will fly skyward, symbolizing peace and love.

The principles of past-life therapy that the leaders of the school teach explain the physics of reincarnation. Guilt, phobias, and emotional reactions are the result of negative circumstances created in some past-life experience, according to their beliefs.

One of my ministry associates, Paul Joiner, visited the offices of the Unarius Academy and was escorted by a grandfatherly gentleman who spoke of his past life as casually as we would tell about a memorable vacation. When Paul commented that he had heard that Ruth Norman had died, his guide said, "Oh no, she has just gone to the next journey."

Are these beliefs just the aberrations of gullible people who would accept anyone who offered them a feeling of belonging to something important? I think not. In a more sophisticated, subtle form, reincarnation and past-life therapy are being embraced by educated, church-going citizens.

In America, 23 percent of our citizens say they believe in reincarnation. That's one-fourth of our population. If you survey the college-age population (ages eighteen to twenty-four) the proportion jumps to 30 percent. Seventeen percent of those who attend church regularly believe in reincarnation. Twenty-one percent of the Protestant population and 25 percent of the professing Catholic population believe in reincarnation.[3]

Can we really believe that it's "not around here"?

A Matter of Lives and Deaths

Alternative Spirituality is not something "out there"; it touches us here and now. If you go to a therapist, instead of being asked about your childhood, you may be quizzed on the life you led in another place or another era. There are many godly Christian counselors who help people with biblical counseling, but past-life-regression therapy is harmful and contrary to God's Word.

This story appeared in the *San Diego Union-Tribune:*

> Therapists are looking back farther and farther these days, and many of them are astounded by what they see.
>
> It is possible, they say, that today's physical and emotional problems can have roots dating back hundreds and thousands of years.
>
> The idea isn't a new one. Many religions—including Hinduism and Buddhism—and New Agers embrace the premise that the spirit doesn't die but comes back again and again in different bodies and that spirit may carry with it the bad karma left over from unresolved conflicts in former lives.
>
> *But now,* a Yale-educated psychiatrist, Dr. Brian Weiss, who calls himself "the original skeptic" is joining in, lending credibility to the growing past-life therapy movement. (emphasis mine)[4]

Weiss and other professionals are now practicing therapies that intend to unearth the reasons that you or I might have certain phobias or fears.

One woman who was hypnotized by Weiss flipped back about four thousand years. "She recalled events from an earlier life in which she said she drowned in a flood as her baby was torn from her arms by the forces of the water. The woman went on to recall several other past lives, which provided further explanation for her phobias. Her symptoms began improving, and within a few months she was cured."[5]

While we cannot know the reasons this woman felt she had recovered, we do know that her healing could not be attributed to her past life. Perhaps it was the suggestion of the therapist, perhaps it was the result of a hypnotic trance, or it may have been totally demonic!

My Southern California backyard is blooming with the New Spirituality. Willard L. Johnson, associate professor of religious studies at San Diego State University, has studied Asian, Indian, and Native American religions, all of which include the idea of past lives. In answering the statement that reincarnation can't be scientifically proven, Johnson is quoted as saying, "They're part of the spiritual experience rather than part of the physical experience."[6]

Johnson is right about this. Not only is reincarnation in its purest form unsupportable by the scientific method, it is actually refuted by it. Given the number of people who have actually lived since the beginning of time, there is no scientific tolerance for the outlandish claims of multiple reincarnations.

Reincarnation Reviewed

Not many schools teach Latin anymore. It may be a dead language, but it gives us the root meaning of many words. The word *reincarnation* comes from the combination of Latin words *re* and *incarnate*, which mean to come into the flesh again. It is the belief that the soul or some individualized power passes after death into another body. There are all kinds of reincarnation beliefs in addition to the transmigration and reincarnation belief of Buddhists and Hindus. L. Ron Hubbard, founder of Scientology, suggests that one can reincarnate from life forms on other planets. *(Who was E.T. in his previous life?)*

As we mentioned before, Hinduism teaches that life is essentially one: that plants, animals, and human life are so interrelated that souls are capable of "transmigrating" from one to another. A Hindu believes that "every living being at the time of death is reborn in a different form, either higher or lower, whether as a human being, an animal, a heavenly being, or a hell-dweller, and from that state he will again be reborn, and so on endlessly."[7]

Eastern reincarnationists desire moral, spiritual, and, in some instances, bodily perfection, but they believe that one lifetime is not enough to reach that perfection. In some form or another, the self is in a continual wheel of rebirth.[8]

It reminds me of the television show *Wheel of Fortune:* Round and round I go, and where I stop, nobody knows.

Caryl Matriciana, who grew up in an aristocratic family in India, tells the story of walking through the streets of Calcutta with her mother and seeing a place called a "rat temple."

A god was said to have returned as a rat in one of his reincarnations, so bowls of fresh milk were put out daily for the thousands of rats who were breeding in the infested temple. Although milk was too expensive for the lower-class masses to afford, the believers made sure the sacred rats were fed.[9]

Most American reincarnationists are uncomfortable with the transmigration of souls from one species to another. We hear very little of souls moving from human to less-than-human forms. In fact, some of the more well-known believers relate rather exotic past lives. Shirley MacLaine told *Time* magazine that she was "a former prostitute, my own daughter's daughter, and a male court jester who was beheaded by Louis XV of France"—all in past incarnations that she believes she has rediscovered with the aid of mediums, meditation, and, in at least one case, acupuncture.[10]

The quote about being her own daughter's daughter puzzled me. She believes that one of her lifetimes ended when she, as a young woman with a daughter, died. Then when her daughter had a daughter, she was reincarnated again as that daughter. So, in a sense, she became her own granddaughter! How can I comment on that? It took me long enough just to figure it out!

Reincarnation and the Bible

Dick Sutphen, New Age seminar leader, author, and business-man, is an outspoken advocate of reincarnation. He has an organization, Reincarnationists, Inc., "for the purposes of educating and promoting peaceful planetary transformation through an understanding of the principles of reincarnation and karma."[11]

Sutphen was brought up by parents who were members of the Presbyterian Church, although he later became a Unitarian before he rejected Christianity entirely. He believes that human life is not an accidental evolution but that there is meaning and a plan to life.

While Sutphen is a million miles from biblical truth, what he says about meaning and purpose in life sounds almost Christian. Like many tenets of the New Spirituality, his conclusions are incorrect because they are built upon a faulty foundation. There are some who have gone beyond Sutphen to attempt to prove this system of thought from the Bible.

Two passages in the Bible are frequently quoted to try to support the reincarnation view. One is the argument that the Bible teaches the law of karma in stating that we "reap what we sow." Some reincarnationists interpret this as meaning that such results could occur in another life.

Jesus did teach that our present actions have future conse-quences, but He never taught the doctrine of karma. When Paul gave God's warning in Galatians 6:7 ("Do not be deceived, God is not mocked; for whatever a man sows, that he will also reap"), he was referring to the one lifetime we have on earth, not mul-tiple lifetimes.

Some reincarnationists claim the Bible agrees with them because John the Baptist was Elijah reincarnated. This idea is based upon the following passage:

And His disciples asked Him, saying, "Why then do the scribes say that Elijah must come first?"

Jesus answered and said to them, "Indeed, Elijah is coming first and will restore all things. But I say to you that Elijah has come already, and they did not know him but did to him whatever they wished. Likewise the Son of Man is also about to suffer at their hands." Then the disciples understood that He spoke to them of John the Baptist. (Matt. 17:10–13. See also Matt. 11:14 and Mark 9:11–13)

How do we answer that assumption? First, in order for reincarnation to take place, the first body has to die. In 2 Kings 2:9–18, we learn that Elijah never died but was taken to heaven, mysteriously and dramatically, in a fiery chariot. How, then, could he be reincarnated?

In the minds of the Jewish delegation who questioned John, Elijah was associated with the coming of the Messiah. In John 1:21, John the Baptist is asked if he is Elijah, and he answers, "I am not." That's pretty clear.

The Christian Alternative to Reincarnation

To present a case that is plausible to a jury, the defense must have some solid information. Here are four provable facts:

    1. *The process of reincarnation cannot cleanse us from our sins; only the person of the Lord Jesus Christ can do that!*

"Who being the brightness of His glory and the express image of His person, and upholding all things by the word of His power, when He had *by Himself purged our sins*, sat down at the right hand of the Majesty on high" (Heb. 1:3, emphasis mine).

    2. *The process of reincarnation is not my hope for the future; the promises of God are.*

"But if I live on *in the flesh*, this will mean fruit from my labor; yet what I shall choose I cannot tell. For I am hard pressed between the two, having a desire to depart and be with Christ, which is far better" (Phil. 1:22–23, emphasis mine).

    3. *The process of reincarnation is in direct opposition to the doctrine of Christ's bodily resurrection.*

The resurrection of Jesus Christ is the guarantee that we shall also be resurrected someday. "I have hope in God, which they themselves also accept, that *there will be a resurrection of the dead,* both of the just and the unjust" (Acts: 24:15, emphasis mine).

4. *The process of reincarnation does not do away with the judgment in the future.*

"And as it is appointed for men *to die once,* but after this the judgment" (Heb. 9:27, emphasis mine).

Good Karma, Bad Karma

When Malibu, California, was devastated by fierce fires and subsequent mudslides in 1993, it was reported that some people said, "It was just bad karma." What triggered the destruction of millions of dollars' worth of valuable beachfront property? An act of God, a pyromaniac, faulty wiring, or some wicked deed in a person's former life?

To the Hindu or the Western New Ager, karma is an irrevocable law that says everyone gets what he or she deserves. According to the law of karma, there is a general operating principle in the natural world that creates debits or credits based upon personal behavior. These points that are accrued in this life determine each person's fate in the next life. Karma is like a universal bank where we deposit and withdraw. Evil is always punished in the life to come; good is equally rewarded in the life to come.

Karma and the concept of reincarnation are Siamese twins that cannot be separated.

Karma is what is happening to you right now. If your house burned to the ground in the Malibu fires, it was bad karma. If your business fails, it may be the result of your dishonesty in some past life. It's like this: steal the crown jewels in Europe in the eighteenth century and you may be punished in Malibu in 1993.

Past-Life Therapy

If you had lived in another life, how would you know if there wasn't some way to go back and retrieve information about your past? It would be like having a computer that erased every document as soon as you typed it.

For a person to understand what has happened to him or her, the person would have to go through an experience like the woman who went to her therapist and flipped back four thousand years when he asked her to go back into her history.

In their book *The Reincarnation Sensation,* Norm Geisler and J. Yutaka Amano tell the story of a housewife (we'll call her Lorraine) who first went to a past-life-recall therapist because she felt "blocked up" in her everyday life, extremely busy and pulled in a dozen directions. (How many women who don a dozen hats in their daily lives feel the same way?) Lorraine was feeling resentful of all the demands made upon her, and she wasn't able to commit her life and full energy to anything. When she went to a past-life therapist, he induced hypnosis in the sessions. She said of her experience: "I was a man, a member of the Sanhedrin, the leaders of the Jews before the time of Christ. It was horrifying. We were misleading the Jewish people. They were being led to believe that we knew the nature and will of God, and we didn't. In fact, we were working hand in hand with the Roman government in taxing the people. . . . I was caught in it, did not know how to get out of it. I felt a lot of ambivalence, a lot of self-hatred."

As Lorraine came out of hypnosis she learned that "if I was willing to withhold something important then, and it bothered me, I could do something about it now, not withhold my energy from my present life." She said that the experience freed up the "spiritual blockage" that she had been feeling and was a turning point in her life.[12]

Watch how strategically the enemy packages this experience. Her past-life experience was in a context of biblical knowledge, and yet it was totally taken out of context. She was not a part of the Sanhedrin; nor did she live in the time of Christ. Satan will use anything he can to cloud and confuse our minds to make us embrace doctrine that is not from God.

Then there was the doctor's receptionist who couldn't stand perfume of any kind. She phoned all of the female patients who came to her employer's office and asked them not to wear any perfume when they came for appointments. She was in jeopardy of losing her job, so she went to a therapist. He regressed her through therapy, and she discovered that she was an Eskimo woman in a former life who was raped by a man who put his hand over her mouth so she wouldn't scream. The stench of whale oil, which is the basis for some perfumes, exuded from his hands. The past-life-recall therapist claimed that once she understood why perfume disgusted her, it would never bother her again.

In the medium-sized town (and that's not meant to be a pun) where I live, these techniques are widely used.

The Unarius Academy has a book on its list of publications called *The Principles and Practice of Past-Life Therapy* written by Ruth Norman and Charles Spagle. This is the advertisement for that book:

> Here, for the first time, is the record of a sixteen-week Seminar of the Principles and Practice of Past-Life Therapy. This is undoubtedly the most authoritative account of a subject that has boggled and intrigued some of the greatest scientific minds: the mystery of the Continuity of Consciousness as it crosses the barriers of time and space.

The advertisement continues by saying that the Unarius Academy has pioneered the teaching of past-life therapy for thirty-seven years. In one class session, it says, sixty-four students related accounts of healings that resulted when they successfully located the past-life cause of their present emotional problems.

The academy claims to answer this important question: *What is my spiritual identity, and how can I attain peace of mind?*

Road to the Past

How can people get in touch with their past lives, according to reincarnationist doctrine? There are several ways, and one of them is *intuitive recall.* We have all experienced déjà vu at some time or another. We know that intuitive recall can be explained by simply pointing out that when you think you've been somewhere before or think you have met a person before, you're simply experiencing an attempt on the part of your subconscious mind to relate the present experience with something you really have experienced in the past.

For instance, you may have seen a photograph of a person or place, and although you can't consciously remember having seen it, your subconscious mind relates an encounter you may have had with a similar person or place. You may have the feeling that you have seen something before, but that has nothing to do with your having lived a past life. Would you want to base your entire eternity on something as flimsy as that?

Some believe they can discover their past through *psychic recall*. This may be experienced in the office of a psychotherapist, a spiritist, or perhaps a hypnotist. The person is put into a trance and loses control of his or her thinking processes. Whenever anyone gives the control of his or her mind to another, that person opens himself or herself to demonic intervention.

The basic flaw in intuitive or psychic recall as proof for reincarnation is this: *The knowledge of past events does not imply one's presence in those events.* It is possible to have accurate knowledge of past events without having been there personally. Even honest reincarnationists will admit to this. The most likely explanation for this phenomenon is not the transmigration of souls but the transmigration of demons.

Take a Trip

Reincarnationists have gone into the travel business. *Newsweek* magazine reported the entrepreneurial endeavors of Déjà Vu Tours based in Berkeley, California, which specializes in "spiritual adventure" travel. Here's the itinerary:

> [Déjà Vu Tours] boasts that its clients have "seen the sun rise at Stonehenge, visited the Room of the Spirits at the Dalai Lama's Monastery, participated in rituals led by a shaman at Machu Picchu, sung a greeting to the Kumari, the Living Goddess of Nepal, and received baptism in the Jordan River." Susan Hull Bostwick, who started Déjà Vu Tours 13 years ago, says her clients are *people who have a*

sense that they've lived before and want to stand in the sacred places of their past. (emphasis mine)[13]

When I hear all the ways people get involved in regressing to their past lives, my question is, "Why would anybody get into this?" Many people tell us they can't believe in the Bible or the deity of Christ, His death and resurrection, because it takes too much faith. However, it takes an incredible amount of blind faith to believe in reincarnation.

What's the Attraction?

One of the questions that comes to our minds as we are introduced to this subject is, "Why would any thinking modern person be tempted to believe in reincarnation?" As you remember from statistics, reincarnation belief is on the rise.

I was on an airplane going to a speaking engagement and hoped to use the time to study for the message I would give the following Sunday at my church. I spread my notes on the tray table and began studying, conscious that the man next to me kept glancing over at my writing. Finally he asked me what I was studying.

"I'm going to speak at my church next Sunday on reincarnation."

He nodded his head affirmatively and said, "Oh, that's wonderful! It's helped a lot of people."

He must have thought I was going to give a positive report on reincarnation. That's the way many think about it: *If it helps you, that's important.* Buy into it, and let it do its thing. No doubt your neighbors and mine believe in reincarnation for what seems to be good reasons.

I explained to him that I did not believe in reincarnation: I believed in eternal life, which is far better. I showed him the verse in Hebrews 9:27 that says "it is appointed for men to die once, but after this the judgment."

After my brief conversation on the airplane, I wondered, *Why is this belief growing?* We know it is seeping into every corner of our society, but the only reason we don't know how fast it's growing is because we can't get our arms around it. There is no way to track it. However, people are pulled in because it's what they believe is a wonderful way to deal with life.

First, it's an *escape from death*. The Bible says that many people go through life in fear because they are in bondage to death. If you believed in reincarnation, you wouldn't have to worry about dying. Reincarnation is Satan's major lie to deal with the problem of death. Remember what Satan told Eve in the Garden? "You will not surely die" (Gen. 3:4). The reincarnationist believes you'll just check out of this life and start over in a new life.

Do we face the fact that death is a reality? That's the question in the heart of every human being, whether or not the person wants to admit it. George Bernard Shaw wrote with a wry wit, "The statistics on death are quite impressive. One out of one people die."

Billy Graham said in his book *Facing Death and the Life After*, "The truth is that all of us have our time to die, and the conspiracy of silence that so often surrounds death today cannot change that fact. . . . Within most of us is a strong desire to hold on to physical life as long as possible."[14]

Reincarnation purports to take the fear out of death.

Next, reincarnation provides an *excuse for sin*. It is appealing to a lot of people because it allows them to continue living the way they are without ever having to deal with their sin and helplessness before God. Why should you feel personally accountable if you have the opportunity to go around one more time, trying to get it right? For instance, if a reincarnationist is pursuing an immoral lifestyle, he or she doesn't have to deal with the consequences because it's not his or her fault. It is the result of something that happened in the past, and this person is just living out his or her karma.

I have heard the most bizarre things about how movie stars who are into reincarnation explain their adulterous affairs. They say they were really married in a past life to the person with whom they are committing adultery. Now the past-life husband (or wife) has migrated into their present lover's body, so they are having a reunion from a past-life relationship. (How do they celebrate wedding anniversaries? "We just had our twenty-fifth hundredth anniversary!")

Third, reincarnation supposedly has a great *explanation for evil*. The principle of karma answers the question of suffering and evil in each person's life. Everyone is suffering what he or she deserves. If you are suffering, it is because you did something worthy of suffering when you lived before. This doesn't solve the problem of why people suffer.

As a pastor I am with many people who have tragic circumstances in their lives. Can you imagine what it would be like if a reincarnationist sat at the bedside of a child who was dying with cancer and said to the parents, "I know this is really hard for you, but don't worry about it. Don't blame God; He is not involved. What is happening to your child right now is the result of something that was done in a previous life."

The reincarnation issue is dangerous because it doesn't have the answer to suffering, evil, or life after death. It leaves a person with little hope for today or the future.

So Be Forewarned!

Life is cheap among the masses of reincarnationists.

A visit to India should convince us that the land of predominant Hindu belief is impoverished and starving. Sacred cows roam the streets while diseased and maimed beggars plead throughout every town and city.

God puts more value on *one* human life than on the whole world. "For what will it profit a man if he gains the whole world, and loses his own soul?" (Mark 8:36). Read it again. It doesn't say *souls*.

The importance of this present life is not one of countless reincarnations to be quickly ended, to get it over with and get on to the next. In this present life, we determine where we are going to spend eternity. If we have the idea that this life is no big deal, that if we mess it up we have another chance, then we're off the track and headed for collision with the Word of God.

Reincarnation pushes people into psychic encounters with demonic forces.

Terri Hoffman headed an organization called the Conscious
Development of Body, Mind, and Soul, Inc., in Dallas. She began teaching small classes where half of each session was spent
in group meditation. One former student said, "Terri would talk
about reincarnation and about how to become more spiritually
developed." She said she was given special knowledge about previous lifetimes and other planes of existence where, she claimed,
humans ascend after death.

"Over a 12-year period, 10 people with close ties to Terri
Hoffman met untimely deaths through suicide, accident, or,
possibly, murder. Several of them left money and valuable property to her."[15]

It was reported in the October 1990 issue of *Good Housekeeping* that Terri and her organization were also under criminal
investigation by the Dallas County district attorney's office.

What forces were at play in this woman, who claimed to
have been given special knowledge about previous lifetimes and
other planes of existence, that led to these tragedies?

The only way to regress into other lives is to go to a therapist, a psychic, or a spiritist who in some way induces a state of
mind where a person does not have full control.

Whenever you are tempted to consult some "spiritual ad-
viser" who does not believe in the Scripture and does not have
a personal relationship with Jesus Christ, just remember some
of these warnings:

"Give no regard to mediums and familiar spirits; do not
seek after them, to be defiled by them: I am the LORD your God"
(Lev. 19:31).

"A man or woman who is a medium, or who has familiar
spirits, shall surely be put to death; they shall stone them with
stones. Their blood shall be upon them" (Lev. 20:27).

According to 2 Kings 23:24, consulting mediums increased
in a time of rebellion and idolatry. However, when Israel experienced revival and restoration, the spiritists, mediums, and idols
disappeared.

We can look at America today and say that a spirit of rebellion is sweeping our land. In a post-Christian culture, anything
goes, including moral bearings. There is no other explanation

for the growth of the New Spirituality than the defiance or ignorance of God's Word.

Reincarnation presents the false hope of a second chance.

Reincarnation is a system of moral evolution. As a person goes through a countless number of alleged lives, moral issues need not be resolved here and now. You can get to them later.

Christ taught that people decide their eternal destiny in this one lifetime. One of His followers wrote the teaching I cited to my fellow airplane passenger, "And as it is appointed for men to die once, but after this the judgment" (Heb. 9:27).

It is important to decide for or against Jesus Christ here and now. If you were the adversary, wouldn't it be a master stroke to deceive mankind into believing there is no real problem? If you have all of this life and as many other lives as you need to get it right, there is no urgency to decide about your own eternity.

If it were true that there were other lives in which we could get right with God, isn't it rather unloving of Jesus not to let us know? Instead, He told this story, recorded in Luke 16, to make His point clear: There was a rich man and a beggar named Lazarus. The poor man died and was carried by the angels to Abraham's side. The rich man also died, and in hell he called for Lazarus to comfort him. The agony in the fire of hell was so intense the rich man begged Father Abraham to send Lazarus to just dip the tip of his finger in water and cool his tongue. But communication and action were impossible because there was a great chasm between them and no one could cross over from one place to the other.

The rich man then pleaded with Abraham to send Lazarus to warn his brothers about the horrors of hell. But Abraham replied, "They have Moses and the prophets; let them hear them."

The rich man cried, "If one goes to them from the dead, they will repent."

Abraham told the rich man that if his brothers wouldn't hear Moses and the prophets (if they didn't believe the truth in the Scriptures) they wouldn't be persuaded by anyone who arose from the dead.

We do not have a second chance; the Bible teaches that we have one precious life. That life is a wonderful stewardship and trust that has been given to us from God, and while we live on this earth one time, God wants us to bring honor and glory to His name and to live in such a way that we will be a reflection of who He is in our lives.

Any of us, in a moment's time, could stand before God and give an account of our lives and who we are. You want to live again? Jesus is the One who has all the answers that the reincarnationist doctrine can never resolve. He put His foot on the neck of death and destroyed its power. When you put your trust in Christ, you will live forever in His presence.

Reincarnation is just one of the old beliefs that the New Spirituality is rejuvenating. It is joined by other fellow travelers in the subversion.

4

THE FORCE

A FEW YEARS AGO WORDS LIKE *channeling, altered states of consciousness,* and *psychic healing* were unknown to us. However, in the decade of the eighties they became as common as fast food. It took generations for America to shift from theism to humanism but only a brief time to embrace the New Spirituality.

Lisa Baker (not her real name) was a member of the "baby buster" generation, those who were born between 1965 and 1983. She told a member of the Barna Research Group her story:

> "I grew up in a very religious home. My parents made us go to mass every Sunday. Once I turned eighteen, that was it. I haven't been back to the Catholic Church since. I have visited a bunch of other churches, to see what they're about. It's been interesting, but I still haven't found the answer."

> Lisa, like many of her generation, is still searching for "the answer." Disenchanted with much of what life has thrust in her path, she is seeking understanding about her purpose, about the reason for pain and suffering, and for the answers to other challenging questions.

> The mainstream faiths have been a disappointment to her: "I honestly tried them. They just couldn't speak to me."[1]

Who or what will fill the spiritual void in the life of some-one like Lisa? Or in the lives of millions who have chosen to ignore the church and find spiritual reality elsewhere?

Waiting in the wings, ready to perform for many spiritual seekers, are those persons who are really occultists (although most would reject that label). Those who are involved with me-diums, astrology, psychic healing, magic, and various methods of inducing trancelike states of consciousness are influencing millions of Americans.

In C. S. Lewis's fascinating parody *The Screwtape Letters*, he told about conversations Satan had with his workers who were being sent out to try to seduce humans.

> Our policy, for the moment, is to conceal ourselves. Of course this has not always been so. We are really faced with a cruel dilemma. When the humans disbelieve in our existence we lose all the pleasing results of direct terrorism, and we make no magicians. On the other hand, when they believe in us, we can-not make them materialists and skeptics. At least, not yet. I have great hopes that we shall learn in due time how to emo-tionalize and mythologise their science to such an extent that what is, in effect, a belief in us (though not under that name) will creep in while the human mind remains closed to belief in the Enemy. The "Life Force," the worship of sex, and some aspects of Psychoanalysis may here prove useful. If once we can produce our perfect work—the Materialist Magician, the man, not using, but veritably worshipping, what he vaguely calls "Forces" while denying the existence of "spirits"—then the end of the war will be in sight.[2]

Lewis wrote those prophetic words before the New Age movement impacted America, before the New Spirituality gained momentum, and before *Star Wars*. Screwtape (Satan himself) could not blatantly talk about evil, nor allow people to believe in sa-tanic forces or demons. He had to couch his activities in more palatable terms. So he championed worship of "the Force."

Satan, the greatest master of disguises, dons his charming personality and beckoning smile and transforms himself into an angel of light (see 2 Cor. 11:14).

In response to the heresy of his day, the Bishop of Lyons wrote in the second century, "Error, indeed, is never set forth in its naked deformity, lest being thus exposed it should be at once detected. But it is craftily decked out in attractive dress so as by its outward form to make it appear to the inexperienced more true than truth."

One of the forces the Great Deceiver uses to lead people away from the truth is to use a demon to speak through the voice of a human.

The Channeling Epidemic

Channeling is a sophisticated term for spirit possession. It occurs when humans willingly give their minds and bodies to spirit beings that enter and control them. The spirits use the mouths of channelers to give spiritual teachings to the listener. To be a channeler is to be a modern-day demon-possessed person or, in some cases, a plain fraud.

Maybe it would be more pleasing to the American palate if we used acceptable pseudonyms like *spirit guides,* instead of the despicable term *demons.* America is demonized but not in the same way as it is portrayed in the New Testament. It's not the naked, uncontrollable, demon-possessed creature like the man from the country of the Gergesenes who cowered in the tombs (see Matt. 8:28–34) but the well-dressed American who lives in the suburbs or the famous personality who appears in the gossip columns. As researchers John Ankerberg and John Weldon say, "Today's Americans enter into these experiences voluntarily and interpret them as having positive spiritual value. Time and again in the autobiographies of such persons, we discover that the process of spirit possession is an essentially positive, pleasurable, life-changing and power-inducing experience."[3]

Linda Evans, a television star who has been called one of the world's most beautiful women, believes that her emotional security and sense of peace rest in the hands of a channeler.[4]

A teacher told us she listens to a radio station in Los Angeles at midnight and receives counsel from John the Apostle through a special channeler.

When Sharon Gless won an Emmy for her role in the popular TV series *Cagney and Lacey,* she announced that she owed her success to Lazarus, a disembodied spirit channeled to her by Jacques Purcell, a retired Florida insurance supervisor who runs a multi-million-dollar corporation called Concept Cynergy. The corporation is dedicated to making the teachings of Lazarus available to many. He is especially popular among many of the Hollywood movie elite.

In the late 1970s there were two known professional channelers in Los Angeles, although there were hundreds of people doing the same thing but identifying themselves as psychics, mediums, or spiritualists. Ten years later there were more than a thousand who called themselves channelers.[5]

Channelers include clerks, scholars, artists, office workers, truckdrivers, Ph.D.s, scientists, grade-school dropouts, business executives, and housewives. They come from all races, nationalities, cultures, and creeds. Some of these channelers are atheists to begin with, but more of them seem to come from a disillusioned Christian background.

Newsweek magazine reported that American mystic and channeler Kevin Ryerson, "guides his little flock of 'initiates' from Washington and Hawaii and Georgia through 'the ancient art of emotional healing' that has brought them all the way to Egypt."

Deep in the King's Chamber at the Pyramid's center, Ryerson, who channels Aton-Re, a three-thousand-year-old contemporary of King Tutankhamen, "speaking in Aton-Re's oddly affable accent" leads in incantations: "Ommmmmmmmmm . . . Ammmmmmmm-Ra."[6]

When I read that article, I couldn't help wondering how Ryerson knew the accent of someone who lived three thousand years ago.

"If the scene was strange, it's no longer unusual. Ryerson, whose celebrity following includes actress Shirley MacLaine, is only one of the many gurus who take Americans abroad to search for the sacred."[7]

Out of the Mouths of Channels

If you were watching someone, let's say it's a man, during a channeling experience, here's what you might observe:

He's beginning to fall backward as if he's in a deep sleep. *Will he fall off that chair?* you wonder.

His face and lips are beginning to twitch as if something is trying to get control of him. *Is he going to have a seizure? I wonder if there's a doctor in the room.*

He's breathing differently now, slower and deeper. He doesn't even look the same . . . his expression is like someone concentrating on a great problem. *Is he in pain?*

Now he's speaking, but it's not like his voice at all. *Is this a ventriloquist's trick?*

He's like a puppet, controlled by some entity from another world who is pulling his strings.

All the innocents who go to a channeler out of curiosity can be absorbed into a black hole of despair just as Alice stumbled through the looking glass into another world.

Channeling can take different forms; one kind may involve complete loss of consciousness, another, only partial. What we need to remember is this: It is clear that whatever power the mediums use comes only as a result of their contact with the possessing spirit. They have no power of their own. The demon takes over their personalities.

Let me share with you the story of Russ Consaul. He is described as a soft-spoken consultant for a bank. His best friend is Samuel, who is encouraging, loving, trusting, and compassionate. But Samuel doesn't exist in flesh and blood; he is a "spirit guide" who communicates through Consaul.

Consaul reaches Samuel by channeling—a process in which the channel, or medium, enters a deeply relaxed and often trancelike state and "tunes into another level of consciousness," much like tuning to a different radio station. The spirit entity then expresses itself through the channel's body, usually in speech or automatic writing.

A picture of Consaul appeared in the *Washington Times* showing a young man with his face scrunched up as though in excruciating pain. He was experiencing the spirit Samuel speaking through him.

The spirit is purported to have lived thousands of lifetimes on this planet and on others. "I exist now in a different frequency, in a different space," Samuel said.

In the newspaper article, Consaul said he has spoken with
Samuel several hundred times, "ever since he broke through his
own grip of fear about the unknown."

Here is a man, son of a Catholic mother and Presbyterian
father, who "grew up in a traditionally religious home" and now
is so convinced of the positive benefits of channeling that he
believes that someday it will have corporate and classroom applications, just as psychology does.[8]

Men and women across this country are willingly allowing
themselves to be inhabited by a possessing spirit. We must not
pass this off as a harmless whim of eccentric people. In most cases
these are ordinary folks who belonged to a church when they were
growing up. Finding no fulfillment there, they sought other
ways. Channeling may seem to be a harmless preoccupation, but
it contains all the elements of the wolf's grandmother-disguise
in *Little Red Riding Hood*.

From Bliss to Death

One of the best-known channelers is J. Z. Knight, a woman
who took her followers from bliss to death. J. Z. is a former cable
TV subscription saleswoman who lives in Yelm, Washington. She
channels Ramtha, a thirty-five-thousand-year-old ascended master. Knight has a Baptist background and "once claimed that she
had read the Bible front to back at least six times."[9]

Just about every biography I have read about someone involved
in channeling will say the person was once part of fundamental Christianity. As a Christian pastor-teacher, my heart is burdened about
this. Who in my church, or other Bible-believing congregations,
might be headed toward some of these practices? I feel the urgency
to warn those who might be susceptible to these false teachings.

Knight described her disillusionment with fundamentalism
this way: "I saw a lot of people condemned because they wore
lipstick . . . or things like that, or because they wore black."
She said she really loved God, and the church's emphasis on fear
dismayed her.

Soon after attending a Baptist revival that frightened her
thoroughly, Knight had what she believes may have been

her first psychic experience. "At an eighth-grade slumber party, she looked out the window to see a huge, pulsating, blood-red object reminiscent of the preacher's warning that when the devil came, the moon would turn to blood."[10]

Ramtha came into Knight's life in 1977 when she and the second of her three husbands were experimenting with crystal pyramids. Believe it or not, they were trying to discover the power of crystals to preserve food. One afternoon Knight looked up and saw what appeared to be someone taking a handful of gold sparkles and sprinkling them from the ceiling. As she continued to stare at this, she saw the sparkles take the transparent form of a bald, warrior-like man nearly seven feet tall.

"I am Ramtha, the Enlightened One. I am here to help you," he told her.

After many encounters with Ramtha and a period of time when she feared that he might be the devil, she came to know, trust, and love him. With Knight's approval, Ramtha began using her as a channel while she was in a trance. The early audiences were small, intimate gatherings in private homes. As the word grew, so did the audiences and distances from which people would come to hear Ramtha speak.[11]

Knight became a part of the Hollywood "in" group. Ramtha's disciples were big names in movie circles—Shirley MacLaine, Linda Evans, and Burt Reynolds, to name a few—and as the "wisdom" of Ramtha was spread abroad, the attendance at her seminars increased. Knight became a wealthy woman.

In 1986, the *New Age Journal* described what it was like to see J. Z. Knight channel Ramtha. It said she would be visibly transformed from a fragile feminine personality to a masculine, authoritative individual. Seated in a luxurious chair, surrounded by flowers, she would become very still and begin to breathe deeply. Then her face and entire body would contort and her head would toss about for a few seconds. Strange, growling sounds would accompany the transformation. Then she would stand erect and begin to speak in a masculine tone with a nondescript accent. Ramtha had arrived! She was able to sustain her energy while channeling Ramtha for many consecutive hours without any signs of fatigue.[12]

Is it dangerous? Should we assign channeling to the scrap heap of discarded junk? Listen to what happened a few years after Knight and Ramtha's rise to fame and fortune: J. Z. Knight established the Ramtha School of Enlightenment at her estate near Yelm, Washington. In a setting reminiscent of an English country manor, a new message was being heard. The *Tacoma News Tribune* reported on May 24, 1992, that Ramtha (through J. Z. Knight) used to preach a message of spiritual growth and inner compassion, but now the story changed. "Former students say that the school is steeped in mind control and a terrifying vision of the future. They say it has become secretive and divisive . . . Ramtha has told them their tongues would rot if they spoke to outsiders about the teachings."

Field exercises were conducted in a complex maze of ladders, tunnels, and halls—known as the tank—where it was reported, "There have been people who have had heart attacks, broken arms, broken noses, broken legs . . . if someone got hurt, they'd be put in a little go-cart instantly and taken away and no one would even hear their name."

Stories of sleep deprivation, brainwashing techniques, and fear-based teachings were reported. One of these stories described "one woman, a mental health professional in Olympia, [who] signed up with the Ramtha School of Enlightenment in 1988 because she had reached a point where she *longed for more spiritual meaning in her life*. She said she entered the teachings an emotionally healthy person. By the time she left, nine months later, she said she was suicidal. 'It was the most devastating experience in my life. It took me three years to heal'" (emphasis mine).

What happened to the woman who was heralded as the greatest self-help guru in America? People were going to her to fix their businesses, marriages, everything. She was the one who, through Ramtha, could make everything better.

A few years later, fear permeated her teachings. She began to talk of space aliens who were in conspiracy with the U.S. government and who fed on human beings. She called on people to build secret underground shelters stocked with two years' worth of food so they could protect themselves when the aliens invade. She warned of a war over the human race between the aliens who view humans as cattle they have raised and gods from another planet who created people to be their slaves.

Several former students said their lives were enriched by Ramtha's words, but most people said that what they saw happen in just two years time was the downward gravitational pull of evil.

Satan can't even pretend to be good for very long, can he? Sooner or later when he gets control, he drags people down to their baser instincts. Whether it is called upscale channeling or raw demon possessions, he doesn't care. He has one purpose in mind. He wants to destroy and devour everything God wants to make clean and whole.

My co-author was having lunch with her granddaughter, who asked what she was writing. "Today it's about channeling," Carole answered.

Erin, who is eighteen and about to enter college, replied, "All that New Age is eighties stuff."

It's not just Erin's generation that needs this warning; channeling definitely is still with us. It is a deadly pursuit. Solomon said it well: "There is a way that seems right to a man, but in the end it leads to death" (Prov. 14:12 NIV).

Conceivable Explanations for Channeling

Do these people who have spirit guides speaking through them have some special gift others don't have? There are several possible explanations for this phenomenon.

One explanation is that it is *drug induced*. The entities may be products of hallucinations, or their messages may be induced under hypnotic state drugs. Again, hypnosis is a dangerous practice when someone or something is able to control your mind.

A second concept is that channeling is *pure deception*. The entities do not exist, and channelers resort to fakery to stimulate their reality.

Ex-spiritist M. Lamar Keene confessed that for thirteen years he was part of a nationwide network of two thousand phony mediums who traded information about clients as they conspired to cheat them out of millions of dollars. He claimed that massive card files on these people were kept at Camp Chesterfield, Indiana, for the use of mediums. Psychic investigator Allan Spraggett wrote that his visit to Camp Chesterfield, which at the time attracted fifty thousand or more eager pilgrims each summer, exposed him to seances where fraud was "so crude that it was an insult to the intelligence."[13]

One committed follower of J. Z. Knight once said that she saw Knight impersonate Ramtha when she wasn't in a trance. "We thought she did a better job of doing Ramtha than Ramtha. In fact, we couldn't tell the difference."[14]

Another explanation for channeling is the one I would be most likely to hold, and that is *demon possession.*

In an interview on the *Phil Donahue Show,* Shirley MacLaine said, "I'm what you call a good witch." When she began her exploration into Eastern thought, she "tried to keep an open mind" because she found herself confronted with what she earlier would have considered "science fiction or the occult."

Lying Spirits

Spiritist teaching perverts the nature of God. It lies about Christ and distorts the truth about salvation. The Bible clearly instructs man to reject every form of spiritism as something evil. That is why both channeling and following the teaching of channelers are condemned in Scripture as rebellion against God.

A boy king, Manasseh, the king of Judah, was a ruler who practiced soothsaying, used witchcraft and sorcery, and consulted mediums and spiritists. This fellow came from a good family, but he didn't follow his dad's example. The writer of the Holy Scripture says Manasseh did much evil in the sight of the Lord, provoking the Lord to anger (see 2 Chronicles 33).

Today you don't have to go off into the woods to consult with mediums and spiritists. You can turn on your television at almost any time of the day or night and see people you know telling you to call a number for help with your problems. Don't call! You're not going to get any help, and you may get a lot more than you bargained for. Like Judas, who betrayed the Lord, you will wish you could get your money back.

Leviticus 19:21 records these words: "Give no regard to mediums and familiar spirits; do not seek after them, to be defiled by them: I am the LORD your God."

A large percentage of American adults (over 40 percent according to one poll) believe spirits have enabled them to contact the dead. The spirits claim that because they have lived many lifetimes, they have discovered the secrets of life and death.

Spirits also appear in a form that would be most appealing to the spiritual seeker. In their booklet, *The Facts on Spirit Guides*, Ankerberg and Weldon cite some of the astounding shapes the spirits are taking today.

> The spirits claim to be extraterrestrials (including Martians and Venusians), various gods of ancient or modern cultures (or God Himself), Jesus Christ, ascended masters, angels and nature spirits. By doing this, they know they will spark the interest of the people they are contacting. They may also claim to be various aspects of the human mind or the "collective" mind of humanity (some of the terms used here include the Creative Unconscious, the Higher Self, the Oversoul, the Super-conscious Mind, the Universal Mind and the Collective Unconscious). They also claim to be the Holy Spirit, troubled ghosts, the spirits of animals and plants (dolphins, trees, flowers), multiple human personalities, the inhabitants of mythical cultures (Atlanteans, Lemurains), and even a possible alien computer that exists in the future.[15]

If you love science fiction, an extraterrestrial guide may be your choice. Environmentalists will love the dolphin craze. (We are told that a dolphin's sonar can induce a "theta state" in our brainwaves that produces a reaction similar to hypnosis.) Or perhaps your guide will be a bestselling author who uses traditional Christian terms to take you on a spiritual journey.

Demon Activity Fails the Proof Test

Courtroom dramas rivet our attention as prosecution and defense attorneys present evidence for their cases. As onlookers,

we are swayed by the evidence presented for or against the de-
fendant. Many times our prejudices or sympathies are a result
of our own experience. In highly visible trials such as we have
experienced in California in the past few years, it is a challenge
to find impartial jurors.

However, God gives us specific guidelines for determining
whether something is demonic or from God:

> Beloved, do not believe every spirit, but test the spir-
> its, whether they are of God; because many false prophets
> have gone out into the world. By this you know the Spirit
> of God: Every spirit that confesses that Jesus Christ has
> come in the flesh is of God, and every spirit that does not
> confess that Jesus Christ has come in the flesh is not of God.
> And this is the spirit of the Antichrist, which you have heard
> was coming, and is now already in the world. (1 John 4:1–3)

The Bible instructs us to reject every form of spiritism as
something evil. Channeling is a form of spiritual warfare with
the souls of men at stake.

Satan is a great counterfeiter. He wants to counterfeit the
work of the Holy Spirit. Like a prowling lion, he creeps up
alongside of us and says, "Don't let the Spirit of God fill you.
We can show you how to be possessed with a better spirit." One
thing I know about physics is that you can't have space filled to
capacity with two separate entities. If you are filled with the Holy
Spirit, you won't be demon-possessed.

If you are dabbling with spiritism of any type, you don't
have to be under that bondage anymore. If you have any involvement, renounce all demonic activity in your life. I ask you
to return to full and complete dependence upon the shed blood
of the Lord Jesus Christ alone for your salvation. Reclaim the
power of the Holy Spirit to enable you to live your life every
day. He is truly the great possessing Spirit. He is the One who
wants to come and control you.

In Acts 19:19 good advice is given to those who have
turned from spiritism to Christ: "Many of those who had practiced magic brought their books together and burned them in
the sight of all."

My parents were very godly, practical people. They used to say to me, "If it's doubtful, it's dirty." That homespun advice kept me out of a lot of trouble.

Satan wants to deceive you and capture your children. Don't let him do it!

5

RESCUE OUR CAPTIVE CHILDREN

Mommy . . . Mommy . . . Mommeeee . . ." Those shrieks of terror coming from the next room at 1 A.M. hit Mom and Dad like an electric shock. "I'll go," said Mom, stumbling out of bed as if an earthquake had hit. Four-year-old Trudy's wailing was reaching another crescendo by this time. Dad rolled over, remembering his seven o'clock breakfast date with a client. *Just one good night's sleep is all I want. Why does that child have so many nightmares?*

"Now, now, Trudy, it's all right," Mother murmured, hugging the trembling little figure close.

"He was in my room . . . he . . . he was coming to get me," she sobbed.

"There's no one here except you and me, Honey. Now cuddle up and go back to sleep."

As Trudy began to quiet down, she hugged her favorite stuffed animal. No, it's not a teddy bear or a soft doll but a vivid green dragon with black wings and a huge tail with red scales along the sides. It has a lion's mouth, pointy teeth and claws, two glowing red eyes, and a third large green eye in the center of its forehead.

Can you imagine taking your child to bed and saying prayers with him or her, then tucking the little one in to sleep with a dragon? Children have grown to want these ugly, hybrid, mutant, supernaturals on their wallpaper, curtains, lunchboxes, and T- shirts. I saw the sweetest-looking little brother and sister wearing shirts emblazoned with a creature that had fangs, claws, and menacing eyes staring from empty sockets. Whatever happened to Christopher Robin and Winnie the Pooh?

But that's only a small part of what is captivating and capturing the minds and souls of our children today. The world of evil spirits is establishing a beachhead in the toy box.

On television (including cartoons), in movies, and in current children's fiction, occult references are mentioned in spells, magic, pantheism, polytheism, reincarnation, psychic powers, and supernatural forces. These are not like the bad witch and the good fairy godmother within the pages of the brothers Grimm or Hans Christian Andersen. As Bob and Gretchen Passantino wrote in their excellent book, *When the Devil Dares Your Kids*, "They differ qualitatively from the supernaturalism of classic fairy tales, where good and evil are distinguishable, morality is rewarded, and evil ultimately is vanquished by good. Instead, the typical supernaturalism of children's programming promotes relativism, a neutral force or power that can be used either for good or evil."[1]

Danger in the Promised Land

The ancient book of Deuteronomy, written many centuries before the birth of Christ, contains an incredible passage that helps us understand how God wanted to prepare His people for an awesome time in their history. They had been sheltered and sequestered, first as prisoners in Egypt and then as a people wandering in the wilderness. The time had come for them to enter into the land of Canaan, which God had promised to them. The Promised Land! Home. Safe.

Unfortunately, the land was already occupied; it was filled with pagan people. The great concern in the heart of our God was that when His chosen ones entered into the land of Canaan, they would be absorbed into the culture of the Canaanites. They would be like little children, swayed by the prevailing patterns in a pagan society.

God warned them of some real danger ahead. The Israelites had been wandering and living frugally for many years. When they entered this new and wonderful land that had been promised to their forefathers, they were going to experience an abundance of food they had not grown and the luxury of houses they had not built. It was like the rich inheritance we enjoy in America. We haven't traversed mountains and deserts in covered wagons. We haven't cut trees or carved nails to build our own homes. America was given to us to build or destroy.

God warns us, as He did the Israelites:

> Beware, lest you forget the LORD who brought you out of the land of Egypt, from the house of bondage. You shall fear the LORD your God and serve Him, and shall take oaths in His name. You shall not go after other gods, the gods of the peoples who are all around you (for the LORD your God is a jealous God among you), lest the anger of the LORD your God be aroused against you and destroy you from the face of the earth. (Deut. 6:12–15)

Christians are violating the encouragement and instruction of the Lord if, knowingly or unknowingly, they have allowed those gods to be the focus of attention for their children.

In the classic passage on Christian education, God told Moses to write, "You shall love the LORD your God with all your heart, with all your soul, and with all your strength. . . . You shall teach them [the commandments] diligently to your children, and shall talk of them when you sit in your house, when you walk by the way, when you lie down, and when you rise up" (Deut. 6:5, 7).

One of the tasks of being godly parents is that God has put us in charge of being watchmen over our families. We are to diligently look out for the welfare of our children. Appointments with the dentist and the doctor and limiting the candy are not the only responsibilities we have. Piano lessons, soccer games, and even Christian education are unimportant if we lose our children in the world of "fun and games."

John Dvorak, writing an opinion piece for the *San Francisco Examiner,* asked this question:

When trying to understand the mood of the country, its future and its direction, where do you turn?

Many journalists follow the annals of Congress. Others have deep discussion with learned professors. You know where I go? I'll tell you. I go to Toys "R"Us. Here's where the coming generations are molded. Let me tell you, the future die is cast, and the image is a sick one

It is not that the toy business hasn't always been fraught with weird fads, tasteless imagery and warped symbols that have little value, but now it's worse than ever. One is simply overwhelmed by a plethora of toys best described as gruesome, gory and irresponsible.[2]

Although my four children are beyond the age of a visit to the toy store, I decided to go on a little windowshopping trip. I felt like my sensibilities were being hit by creatures from some evil planet. The gamut of games and amusements bombarding our children and young people is so vast and varied that we can only cite some representative areas that should challenge our vigilance. Tucked in with the teddy bears and angora kittens are the dragons and snarling creatures from other worlds. Stacked on the shelves near Monopoly and Scrabble are the leering images of super-biceps monsters wielding guns and swords. Mixed together with NFL games or instructions on tennis are occultic videos. It only takes $1.99 to buy a "collectors pack" of *X-Force*, gruesome comics containing all the monsters and demons kids want to trade with their buddies.

Larry McClain, who authored a book called *Early Earth*, compares today's grotesque toys to the gods of the ancients.

These creatures that show up in archaeology and mythology are not just figments of the imagination. They were literal, physical demonic entities that appeared in civilizations of the past. These types of demagogues, or demonic beings, were represented as part human and part animal in their characteristics like this bird-human of the Assyrians. They can be horse and human-like creatures, fish and human like the god Dagon of the Philistines, part Jaguar part human, but the tongue hanging out over the chin is the universal symbol of demonic possession. And one of the most popular combinations is human and serpent. You can find them on the toy shelves. It is not surprising that pagan religions worshipped serpents and dragons, for the Bible tells us that is exactly what Satan is. He is the Old Serpent and the Dragon.[3]

Someday Satan will be given the key to open the bottomless pit, a place where fallen spirits have been confined. With a burst of smoke, an army of powerful creatures will be released to the earth. Many people believe these are just some imaginary symbols placed in the Bible to startle or frighten us. I believe they will be as hideous as they are described.

The gruesome scenario begins when the bottomless pit is opened and a swarm of locusts emerge "like the smoke of a great furnace." The creatures are commanded to torture everyone who does not have the "seal of God" on his or her forehead. These hideous tormenters will be a terrifying bunch; they will look like horses, have faces like men, hair like women, and teeth like lions. The sound of their wings will be like chariots with many horses racing into battle (see Rev. 9:1–11).

The creatures out of the pit are like the toys in the store I visited! Those people left on earth during the Tribulation will meet these monsters face to face. I have often wondered, as I studied the book of Revelation, how in the world people would see these creatures and not realize something was terribly wrong. Perhaps by the time the world gets to that point, people on earth will be so desensitized to the gruesome images being foisted on them and their children that they won't even get their attention. If you play with the toy all your life then see the real thing, the crossover from imagination to reality is a very small step. This is only conjecture, of course, but no less absurd than what we are seeing in the toy boxes of America.

Larry McClain expressed it this way:

Our generation won't be shocked by the demonic invasion. They are actually anticipating that extra-terrestrial intelligent beings who look very different from us will someday contact the earth and help us with ecological, monetary and political problems.[4]

What's Funny?

One of the most misused words in this era of doublespeak is *comics*. According to Webster, comics are "amusing or intended to be amusing; humorous; funny." As a pastor, it is not a priority item on my study list to gather sermon material from the comics. As a parent with children in their teens and up, I don't see comic books on the coffee table in our house. So I sent my good associate, Paul Joiner, to do some more research for me. He brought me a whole stack of comic books. The pictures were gross, violent, and frightening. I sat at my desk, staring at these abominations and wondering, *Do most parents realize what their children are taking into their minds?*

Here are just a few examples: a monstrous humanoid with fangs was wielding an ax-like instrument dripping with blood. The title was "Youngblood." Another called "Scarlett" (with the t's shaped like daggers) showed a young woman with a gash on her face running from a specter wielding a long sword. One "comic book" had a series of hideous creatures plotting to kill someone. The last caption read, "What's the matter, have you gone soft in your old age? Killing innocent people used to be no problem for you . . ."

Have we reached a stage when we cannot be shocked by anything? How many parents know about these so-called comics that are stashed under the bed? The demons portrayed (and I couldn't call them men) are sinister, their faces contorted in fiendish scowls. Some of them have chains with skulls around their necks and brandish weapons of every description. The subhuman types defy the imagination. Paul wrote me a note that said, "The lady at the children's comic-book store told me that these particular comics are among the most popular. Everyone from kids to adults read the stories and collect these books."

I couldn't understand the strange words in many of them, but one of them I figured out. It was *mantra*. A mantra is a Hindu incantation or prayer. Some of the copy in this comic reads, "The eternal warrior has died many times before. An elite foot soldier in the eternal battle between good and evil has been reincarnated into the never-ending fray over and over again. By this time he has been brought back as a woman permanently. And to make matters worse, her only ally, Warstrike, is the man who killed her in the first place."

Common themes run through these "most popular" comic books: (1) Subtle satanic phrasing, symbols, and terms; (2) Subtle religious phrasings, symbols, and terms; (3) Excessive amounts of blood, violence, demons, and witchcraft; (4) Physical and sexual beauty of the characters—perfect bodies, even of demons and supernatural beings; and (5) Evil appears right, and good has an evil edge to it. Wrong and right are almost indistinguishable.

Where does your child's allowance money go, *Peanuts* or the *Warlock Chronicles?*

But It's Only a Game

There's no doubt that we live in a computer age. One of the things that is a problem now is that kids know a lot more about them than parents. Many of the things that are happening today to inculcate new thinking patterns into the minds of our children are being done through computer games like *Heroes Quest I,* which coaxes, "Create your own character from the ground up. Venture forth into a world of magic. Become a mysterious magician, a fierce fighter or a wily thief."

Ultima—the False Prophet, another computer game, has the picture of a winged demon on the front. Other games a young person might play after school could be *Wizardry, Shadowrun* (Life on the Cyberpunk fringe of the future) or, for more violence, how about *Total Carnage?* Here's the one that contained no hidden agenda: *Psychic World*—"Call on your basic psychic powers to overcome dangerous monsters and deadly machines. Along the way pick up your psychic powers—the powers of ESP can overcome the power of evil." *Phenomenon—The Game That Goes One Step Beyond* promises those who are twelve and older "The Extra Sensory Party." It offers to teach them *telepathy* ("the fun of transmitting images"), *clairvoyance* ("Is what you see what you get?"), *dermal vision* ("seeing" with your skin), and *psychometry* ("Can personal objects reveal your secret past?").

This game's promotion reads: "*Phenomenon* . . . gives you a chance to explore, unlock, and develop your psychic ability during a fun, fascinating game. What's more, you and your friends are doing it together."

There is also one called *Tales of the Crystals*: "A game that changes your home into a world of myth and magic."

In a world that has lost its awe of God and its wariness of His enemy, why not try these games? Why not experiment with anything that offers secret knowledge, thrills, and power? Who worries about consequences in an age that denies sin, guilt, and the sovereignty of God?

By far the most popular of the fantasy role-playing games is *Dungeons and Dragons*. Although some stores, like Toys "R' Us, no longer carry it, there are still many game and bookstores that have it on their shelves. The objective is to maneuver characters through a maze of tunnels (dungeons) filled with ambushes, monsters, and magic in search of treasure. Three or more players can play, with the most important player being the Dungeon Master.

Characters are good and evil, with the more evil and violent ones possessing the greater power and life expectancy. Players earn power based on the number of enemies and monsters they kill. Various aids enable characters to survive: magical weapons, spells, potions, daggers, battle and hand axes, magical tridents, and swords. The game continues endlessly as characters are murdered or grow in power to demigod status.

How seductive is *Dungeons and Dragons*? For convicted killer Sean Sellers, the game further fueled the darkness in his life and led him into the trap of Satan worship and the occult. Sellers started playing with *Dungeons and Dragons* at the age of twelve, and when he was nineteen he was found guilty of killing his parents. The downward spiral for this kid took only five years![5]

Although there is no evidence that involvement with an occultic game causes someone to commit suicide, it can be one of the signs of personal, spiritual, or emotional problems. Sean represents a generation of kids who are susceptible to anything. Lack of hope for the future, the sad condition of our society, broken homes, disillusionment with God, the search for personal power, and the desire to be someone special are just some of the factors that were mixed into Sean's life to make the dark side of life appealing.

Jeffrey was an outstanding freshman in a rural high school in Kansas. He was class representative to the student council and played on the junior varsity football team. He was an average kid who showed no signs of despondency or other special problems until one day when he shot himself in the head. His obsession with *Dungeons and Dragons* was a clue that he was a desperate young man. He had become so consumed with the game that he wanted to go to the fantasy world inhabited by other-worldly beings, instead of facing the real world. It led to his death.[6]

Many fantasy role-playing games have taken the nation by storm since they were first introduced into our culture in 1975. Beginning as a fad among college students, the games soon infected impressionable teens and preteens. Still, some people have asked me, "Why are they really so wrong?"

The issue is that players must use vivid imaginations to assume the role of one of the game's characters, many of whom are evil people, thieves, assassins, and users of magic methods. Through the course of the game, which could last for days, weeks, or even months, the player begins to identify more and more deeply with the character. Such intense exposure to the evil intents of these people begins to open up the young person to satanic influence.

I'm not on a witch hunt. I'm not saying to throw away all toys, computer games, or board games. However, if they have occultic or demonic overtones, find a replacement. Too many parents sit back and say, "I don't think my child will be affected by this." We underestimate the forces that may be working on the mind of the child.

Our Christian kids may be the most vulnerable to satanic influence. Steve Russo, who co-authored *The Seduction of Our*

Children, talked with a public school counselor about the increasing problem of students dabbling in occult practices on her campus. "I asked her to give me a profile of the typical young person who is involved in the occult. 'Oh, that's easy, Steve,' she responded. 'They're all church kids. They've had just enough of a taste of the supernatural to make them curious.'"[7]

Just because our kids go to Sunday school or are enrolled in a Christian school doesn't mean they are immune. So what can we do?

1. *Study the New Spirituality and its roots in the New Age movement.*

We certainly don't want to get absorbed in it or the negativity of its input will influence our attitude. However, when I started talking and writing about this, many people in my own congregation came to me and said they had known something was wrong but they hadn't known what it was. It was like trying to find the source of an unpleasant smell. This helped me realize how important it is that we not be ignorant of Satan's devices.

When we understand the foundation and philosophy behind the New Spirituality, we will have the ability to smoke out about 90 percent of its followers' devices.

2. *Selectively monitor your child's television and movie viewing.*

Although we haven't tackled television, it should be apparent that Christian parents face a pervasive foe in the screen. We used to think the safest time in the whole week was Saturday morning. No more!

Television gives a distorted view of the world that children tend to accept. The younger the child, the less able he is to evaluate what he sees or hears. What are the messages? If you don't like someone, you shoot him. It's okay to be sassy to Mom and Dad. Men and women do funny things in bed. Grownups drink beer to have fun.

Using TV as a baby-sitter is dangerous. When the kids are little, turn it off or find good videos such as those from Focus on the Family. When they are older, help them with discernment and discuss the evil values versus God's standards.

At this writing, the "in" thing is *Mighty Morphin Power Rangers*. The "Power Rangers" are five teenagers who "morph" into space creatures to fight the evil invading forces. When my co-author visited a large toy store, she talked with the manager about the phenomenon that has created the biggest toy craze since the Cabbage Patch dolls. The Power Rangers paraphernalia comes in everything from dolls to lunchboxes, and the demand is so high that when it was rumored that one store was receiving a shipment, three hundred people were lined up at the doors when it opened.

The toy-store manager said her son was an avid fan. When he first started watching the television show, he had nightmares and now his daytime playing involves karate chopping and jumping at people.

Children at an impressionable age may internalize what they see and hear and never talk about it, but it's going into their systems. We may wonder two or three weeks later why they are having nightmares and can't sleep.

3. *Scrutinize the things your kids are reading and the games they are playing.*

We think that if they are in a Christian school, the things they get are okay. Although I have a lot more confidence in the Christian schools than I do in the secular, it is never wise to turn off our vigilance. Kids meet other kids, and not everything they bring home was given to them by the school. Sometimes they exchange comic books or Mighty Morphin Power Ranger paraphernalia.

We should not turn off our vigilance sensors. It's like the market that displays fresh vegetables next to rat poison. Even a little taste of the latter could be fatal. The customer makes the choice.

4. *Search the Scriptures, and help your children do the same.*

We must teach our children how to test what they see and hear against the Scriptures. In my book, *Exposing the Myths of Parenthood*, I said:

> Kids today learn a lot about getting to the moon, but very little about getting to Heaven. They can master the intricacies

of the computer better than most adults, but do not know how to explore "the depth of the riches of the wisdom and knowledge of God" (Romans 11:33). They may think the Rock of Ages is a new singer.

We are rich in Bible teachings today. Unlike a few generations ago when the King James Version of the Bible was the only source for Christian learning, now we have children's illustrated Bibles, video tapes, audio-cassettes, vacation Bible schools, puppet shows, records, and concerts. This Christian cafeteria is so full of a variety of food that there's no excuse for parents today not to introduce their children to nutritious spiritual food.[8]

5. *Seek God's help.*

When we walk and pray or sit and pray, we must pray for protection against the inroads that Satan is making through the range of toys, books, and games. We have never had a time in our history when the powers of evil have been fighting so hard to kidnap our children's minds. But our God is stronger, and His Book is the sword our children need for protection.

"The whole Bible was given to us by inspiration from God and is useful to teach us what is true and to make us realize what is wrong in our lives; it straightens us out and helps us do what is right. It is God's way of making us well prepared at every point, fully equipped to do good to everyone" (2 Tim. 3:16 TLB). The apostle Paul certainly recognized the problems and needs of his day when he wrote that "the Lord is faithful, who will establish you and guard you from the evil one" (2 Thess. 3:3).

We need to be *well prepared at every point,* especially as we entrust the lives and minds of our children to the schools!

6

SCHOOLS UNDER SIEGE

SCHOOL DAYS, SCHOOL DAYS, GOOD OLD Golden Rule days. Readin' and writin' and 'rithmetic, taught to the tune of a hickory stick . . ." That song from days gone by is just as antiquated as Mr. Ford's horseless carriage.

What has happened to those basic educational skills every child should have? A U.S. Department of Education survey reveals that two-thirds of our high school students cannot read at their own grade level. Many graduated without being able to write a letter or fill out a job application. The 1993 U.S. Department of Education survey reports that ninety-three million Americans are functionally illiterate. Many educators in the public school system are force-feeding our children with an agenda that promotes a New Spirituality while our basic literacy rates continue to plummet.[1]

A leading humanist spokesman, John Dunphy, sounded the trumpet that preceded the New Spirituality wave in education:

> I am convinced that the battle for humankind's future must be waged and won in the public school classrooms by teachers who correctly perceive their role as the proselytizers of a new faith: a religion of humanity that recognizes and respects the spark of what theologians call divinity in every human being. These teachers must embody the same selfless dedication as the most rabid fundamentalist preachers.

> The classroom must and will become an arena of con-
> flict between the old and the new—the rotting corpse of
> Christianity, together with all its adjacent evils and misery,
> and the new faith . . . resplendent in its promise.[2]

The humanists' modus operandi could not be stated any
clearer: Christianity is decaying, and it must be replaced with
new faith to instill in our children.

Children fed a constant diet of disguised humanistic, occultic,
and spiritualistic ideas in school will more easily accept blatant anti-
Christian rituals as they get older. One example of the Trojan horse
in the schoolhouse is to disguise Eastern-style meditation with terms
like "centering," "calm-down time," and "focusing." Educators
introduce children to certain techniques supposedly to help them
think better, cope with stress, or relax for greater learning.

Other means are not so innocent-sounding: hypnosis, spirit
contact, casting spells. It was when parents brought me the stories of what their children were getting in the schools near my
home that I realized again that these things were not "out
there"; they are "right here."

"How can I possibly monitor everything my child sees or
hears?" one mother said. "I want to be a responsible parent, but
I seem to be battling so many fronts. As soon as I monitor the
TV, check out the computer games, and watch the comics he
buys, my son comes home from school with some crazy story
about sitting in a circle and imagining that he is floating out of
his spiritual eye and into the leaf of a plant. Has the whole world
gone crazy, or is it just me?"

It's hard to respond to the concerns of parents today because I know what they face. We are in a struggle for the hearts
and minds of our children while the enemy is using the strategy
of subterfuge. It is not my intention to indict the entire public
school system and the many loyal, dedicated teachers, but to
alert parents, grandparents, and all who are concerned about the
future of our country to the inroads the New Spirituality has
made in the classrooms of our nation.

Marilyn Ferguson told us bluntly in *The Aquarian Conspiracy* that of the "Aquarian Conspirators" (her description of

New Agers) surveyed, more were involved in education than in any other category of work. She said, "They are . . . in 'peaceful struggle' within the system. There are heroes in education, as there have always been heroes, trying to transcend the limits of the old structure; but their efforts are too often thwarted by peers, administrators, parents."

We are also told that, "Mario Fantini, former [President] Ford consultant on education, now at the State University of New York, said bluntly, 'The psychology of becoming also has to be smuggled into the schools.'"[3]

"Smuggled?" Is this an educational tool or a drug cartel?

My question is, *what does the "psychology of becoming" want us to become?*

The answer could be multiple choice:

a. Humanism plus *supernatural* power becomes New Age.

b. Hinduism plus *pop psychology* becomes New Age.

c. Pantheism plus confidence in *human potential* becomes New Age.

d. Even *"crossless Christianity"* fits if we subtract its heart—Jesus Christ and His atonement—and then add some Eastern mysticism.[4]

All of the above answers are correct.

Although the proponents of New Age practices in our schools have made extensive inroads since Ferguson revealed their strategy, they should not be given all the credit for the spread of deception. Satan is the author of a subversive plan to set up a global government where he will reign with his puppet, the Antichrist, and he needs to draft as many followers as he can before Christ returns.

Our children are His most valuable recruits.

Behind the Masks

For the safety of our children, we need to know for certain whether they are being exposed to the masks of the New Spirituality and what we can do about it.

We do not need to be confrontational or alienate every teacher and school administrator we encounter, but we do need to know our facts and have a firm foundation in our own beliefs.

By the time we learn about a school program or technique, it may be out and another in its place. It's like the manufacturer who changes the graphics on the cereal box. It looks different on the shelf, but when you taste it, it's the same product.

In his well-documented book, *The New Age Masquerade: the Hidden Agenda in Your Child's Classroom,* Eric Buehrer describes a pilot program called Mission SOAR (Set Objectives, Achieve Results) that was introduced in the Los Angeles Unified School District. The object was to reduce gang violence and build self-esteem. What it did was to introduce children to their very own spirit guides in a lesson called "Rainbow for Relaxation." The intention was to help children relax, which sounded like a good idea on the surface.

The children were told to sit up straight and close their eyes, then the teacher read a story to them that described a guided journey into a land filled with different-colored rainbows. While in an almost hypnotic state, they were told to repeat, "I like myself; I am happy; I am in perfect health; I have full control of myself; I am using more and more of my mind each day."

They were brought out of a trance with the instructions, "You will be wide awake, healthy, full of energy, refreshed, and in tune with life."

The next lesson for the school children after "Rainbow for Relaxation," was called "Workshop and Helpers." In this harmless-sounding program, the children were told that they could build a special house where they could go anytime they wanted and with anyone they wanted. They could have any person come and visit, no matter whether he or she was dead or alive, real or imaginary.

Would we want our children to be taught necromancy—which is an attempt to contact the dead through sorcery? In Deuteronomy 18, God specifically refers to the sin of spiritism, witchcraft, and necromancy.

Setting goals is an admirable trait to teach children, but the SOAR program would lead children through the hypnotic rainbow exercise, help them visualize building their workshop, and then tell them to "get ready to meet your two helpers." The male and female helpers were "behind the sliding door in your elevator. Use the control panel on the arm of your chair to make the door of your elevator open."

When Mary and Johnny, always eager for a different game, were introduced to their helpers, the teacher said, "Your helpers are both experts and can help you, teach you, guide you, listen to you and counsel you at any time."

Buehrer, formerly a high school history teacher and now founder of Gateways to Better Education, received a package, wrapped in plain brown paper, that contained the curriculum of Mission SOAR. A teacher in the Los Angeles school district had sent the material—anonymously, for fear of jeopardizing his teaching position.

After opening the package and reviewing its contents, Buehrer said:

> It is a sad commentary on society when we feel we have reached the desperate point of having to hypnotize young people into good behavior and healthy attitudes. I hardly think that parents send their children to school to undergo such treatment.[5]

Do we want a generation of children growing into adulthood and depending on spirit-guide counsel for their decision making? These children will be our future judges, mayors, governors, and presidents.

This is not a warning for just those who have children in public school; it affects all of us. Mission SOAR may have been removed from the public schools by now due to the work of alert parents; however, Buehrer said, "It is doubtful that New Age educators will cease to press for the infusion of the occult into curriculum."[6]

Buehrer found a close parallel between the hypnotic exercises for children in the Mission SOAR material and a book by leading psychic William W. Hewitt, *Beyond Hypnosis: A Program for Developing Your Psychic and Healing Power.*

Start Them Young

It's like the little girl we'll call Becky, who was excited about kindergarten. She had a new dress, a new lunchpail, and a backpack, just like the big kids. She was always anxious to tell her mother about what happened in school. One day she said, "We did the magic circle again. It's almost like Aladdin. I can go anyplace I want with Muffy."

Mother knew Becky had a great imagination, so she asked, "Who's Muffy?"

"Teacher says we can all have our own special guide who will teach us what we need to know. Muffy is mine."

Special guide? Mother should have had a warning at that point. Have you heard of the "magic circle"? Here are some instructions about this "innocent" little game from a New Age author:

> Whenever you are about to go on a magical journey, or just when you need a feeling of safety and confidence, you can create a magic circle around yourself that will help protect you. To make a protective circle, imagine a glowing ring surrounding you, an energy field that can keep out any harmful energy other people might be directing at you. . . . If you feel you need a companion on your magical journey, you can ask for a spirit guide to appear.[7]

The children move from simple relaxation to guided imagery when the teacher continues to tell them how to picture themselves doing what the teacher describes. "Imagine light coming into your body . . . picture yourself floating in the air or talking to an imaginary animal or person."

The New Spirituality takes guided imagery one step further and moves into a spiritual belief when children are told to meet other beings and find answers for life.[8]

Answers to life are not found in spirit guides but in Jesus Christ, who said, "I am the way, the truth, and the life" (John 14:6).

Recycling Children's Minds

First, I want to make it clear that I am not against environmentalism. We have wasted and spoiled too much of God's glorious creation, and we are facing the consequences.

However, many in the environmental movement worship the creation rather than the Creator. Children are taught to meditate on the earth in this manner:

> Imagine you are the earth, one with Mother Earth. Feel that you are deep inside the center of the earth and that the mountains and oceans and rivers are your body.
>
> Feel all of the rocks as part of you; now feel all of the soil and dirt as part of you . . . now feel all of the little plants as part of you and all of the big trees as part of your body . . . feel that all of the things that live on earth are here to learn and when they finish learning on the school of earth they will enter into the One Source which is beyond the earth but which is always with them . . . let us go deep inside our Source.[9]

During Earth Day celebrations, some schoolchildren wrote poems to Mother Earth and sang "*We've* got the whole world in *our* hands" instead of "*He's* [God's] got the whole world in *His* hands."

Teaching children to be proper stewards of the environment is a Christian value. The Bible says the earth is the Lord's, and as such we should value what we have been given (see Exod. 9:29).

Children should not be taught to spiritualize nature. When spiritual terminology such as "reverence" and "connectedness" are used in our relationship to the earth, it stems from the New Age belief that "all is one," which is pantheism wearing one of its many masks. According to New Spirituality advocates, we must have a relationship with the spirit of the earth.

The psalmist said,

> The earth is the LORD's, and all its fullness,
> The world and those who dwell therein.

For He has founded it upon the seas,
And established it upon the waters. (Ps. 24:1–2)

Self-Esteem or Self-Centered?

The New Spirituality teaches that we must determine our own morality. In our "higher selves," we have the truth; we simply need to listen to our intuition—our sense of what is right.

To give you an idea of what schools have done in the past, there is the influence exerted by the late Dr. Beverly Galyean on three federally funded programs she developed in the Los Angeles public schools. One of her premises was that each child contains all the wisdom and love in the universe. Her philosophy was:

> Once we begin to see that we are all God, that we all have the attributes of God, then I think the whole purpose of human life is to reown the Godlikeness within us.[10]

Hundreds of public school teachers attended conferences led by Dr. Galyean and enthusiastically responded to her ideas. Do you wonder that these ideas have filtered down to our children in the guise of building self-worth?

Messages on self-esteem can be so attractively packaged that even Christian educators sometimes fail to see the New Spirituality influence. A Christian educator in a public school sent me a packet of brochures and tapes by a professional group of New York singers and actors who came to his area. The purpose of the group, called Nu Vision, was to promote self-esteem in the primary schools. The teacher wrote, "After their appearance at my school, upon reflection, the messages that they presented were so subtle regarding self-esteem and being your own 'god.'"

My co-author listened to the tapes from Nu Vision and said the music would appeal to kids, but it wasn't difficult identifying the lyrics. They sang, "Divine power is everywhere," and "The universe is perfect, and so are we."

If we are perfect, why should anyone strive to achieve? This is why this fixation on self-esteem undermines real education.

Let's keep children "feeling good" about themselves, so set the standards low.

Real self-esteem comes when a child learns to master a skill, achieve a goal, and knows he or she is loved unconditionally. A child of God gets his or her self-worth from the knowledge that he or she is precious to Jesus.

We Are the World

When global education is being taught to future teachers in their university classes, it follows that these young college students are going to mold the minds of children into one-worldism. Western Washington University, for instance, offers a course called "Foundations of Education," taught by Professor Philip Vander Velde, coeditor of *Global Mandate,* who uses his book, along with *The Turning Point* by New Ager Fritjof Capra, for his texts.

Future teachers face a curriculum that advocates changing our political structure to socialism and changing their personal religious beliefs to Eastern mysticism. Globalists also train these future teachers about citizenship in a different manner than those of us who are flag-waving Americans would perceive.

The *Global Mandate* states, "Citizenship education, found in every respectable nation claiming to be civilized, is replete with curricula through which it teaches its citizens chauvinism, patriotism and nationalism: the by-products of a world view which pits man against his fellow human beings."[11]

Globalists emphasize the shortcomings of our nation but paint a wonderful vision of the future world society. "Nation-states have outlived their usefulness, and a new world order is necessary if we are to live in harmony with each other. . . . The task of re-ordering our traditional values should be one of the major educational objectives of our schools."[12]

Global Mandate also makes it clear that a new religion, a "global spirituality," is needed to save the world. According to Professor Vander Velde, this spirituality would be a blend of Hinduism and Christianity, which is New Age thinking.[13]

In *The Turning Point,* Capra introduces educators to Eastern mysticism that he claims is now supported by scientists:

As Eastern thought has begun to interest a significant number of people, and meditation is no longer viewed with
ridicule or suspicion, mysticism is being taken seriously even
within the scientific community.[14]

These globalists think Christians are unscientific, back-
wards, and a threat to world unity and peace. In fact, Capra
writes that "Christian fundamentalists promote medieval notions
of reality." His thesis is that if men cling to old religious creeds
(like Christianity) instead of embracing a new faith, world government is doomed.

Globalists are infiltrating the educational system with
world-order workshops at curriculum conferences and social
studies meetings. Are we alert to the methods they use?

Christians, take heed: this is the goal of the globalists:

We have to control church schools because fundamental,
Bible-believing Christians do not have the right to indoc-
trinate their children in their faith, because we, the state,
are preparing all children for the year 2000, when America
will be part of the One World Global Society and their children won't fit in.[15]

That startling comment was made by a state legislator who
appeared on a talk show.

The Great Spirit

Indian lore has always been a fascinating part of our culture. However, all of us, and particularly our children, are
hearing more about Indian spirituality with its practices rooted
in astrology, hypnotic visualizations, sacred circles, magic symbols, and communicating with "wise" spirit beings.

America's growing fascination with the pagan roots of Native American beliefs is seen in movies, television, and books.
Vice President Al Gore wrote in his book *Earth in the Balance*
that "Native American religions offer a rich tapestry of ideas
about our relationship to the earth." He quotes a prayer of the

Onondaga tribe in upstate New York as "another beautiful expression of our essential connection to the earth."

> O Great Spirit, whose breath gives life to the world and whose voice is heard in the soft breeze . . . make us wise so that we may understand what you have taught us, help us learn what lessons you have hidden in every leaf and rock, make us always ready to come to you with clean hands and straight eyes, so when life fades, as the fading sunset, our spirits may come to you without shame.[16]

Indian beliefs and rituals are fascinating, but when children are falsely taught that the Great Spirit and God are merely two names for the same cosmic creator who answers the ritual prayers and meditations of people everywhere, this is universalism and denies all need for the cross.

Too Close for Comfort

It has been said for years that all trends begin on the east and west coasts and converge in the middle. Today I believe that the inroads of New Spirituality, globalism, and all forms of the occult exist from sea to shining sea.

In San Diego and the environs where I live, some of the people in my congregation brought me stories of what our children are experiencing in some of our schools. These examples encompass just a few square miles of our vast country. Multiply them in 3,008 counties and fifty states.

One boy was put into a hypnotic trance by a hypnotist at his public school. They were unable to bring him out of the trance, so they rushed him to the emergency room where the doctor on duty was finally able to help him regain consciousness. The boy has continual nightmares about that occasion.

A high school boy attending a city high school was exposed to palm reading, tarot cards, and a book called *Literature of the Supernatural.* Another boy attended a school where there was much discussion of suicide as well as anti-God, anti-American, and anti-values literature. His mother said, "They robbed my son of any patriotism and subjected him to peer-group pressure because he was a Christian. Today, he continually thinks of suicide."

A nearby school district has been teaching death education that helps an elementary or junior high age student plan his or her death. Students have been told to plan their tombstone statement and write letters to friends. (Family is often excluded from this assignment.) Suicide education at one middle school is so descriptive that students come away with three or four plans that are most often used.

A high school girl was exposed to games where children were forced to pick which parent is to be killed in stories involving both a sinking boat and a fallout shelter. In the sinking-boat exercises, the teacher told the students that old people should be selected to die first.

A young man attends a middle school where meditation and values clarification are taught. His mother told us, "The teachers want to wash his head of all preconceived notions."

A mother told about a school with a pass/fail system in which her nine-year-old boy was passed from grade to grade, even though he was not learning to read. The school refused to keep his parents informed of his failure to learn for fear of hurting his self-esteem. Finally, private specialists decided he had numerous learning disabilities and was at least three years behind other kids his age. He has since been taken out of public school, and his parents are trying to recover the years and educational knowledge he lost.

How has all of this happened in the past few years? We know most of the answers: breakdown of the family, lack of interest on the part of parents, and an educational system permeated by anti-God, New Spirituality thinkers.

Between 1980 and 1990, Sunday school attendance dropped by 33 percent! Public school children are taught that there is no Creator God, that they evolved by accident, and that they, in fact, are their own god. Why, then, should they go to Sunday school?

What Should We Do?

The situation is not hopeless. Most educators are trying to do their best to meet the needs of children and society, but they will teach the curricula given to them without questioning unless parents are informed, organized, and active.

What can you do? First, be informed. What is being taught from the lowest level of schooling through high school? If your small child comes home with stories that make you suspect that guided imagery is being used, check with the teacher and ask him or her to excuse your child from the activity. Get some information from the National Association of Christian Educators, or Gateways to Better Education.[17]

Teachers may innocently use stories about the occult to grab the attention of the class. Provide these teachers information about the dangers in overtly occultic messages without challenging their motives.

If your child is being taught about self-esteem, be sure you understand how this is being approached, and point out to him or her what God sees in each one of us. "You are a very important person because God made only one of a kind when He made you. In the Psalms it says you are 'fearfully and wonderfully made.'

Second, get organized. When parents got together to point out the openly occultic theme in the books called *Impressions,* which were being used by first- through sixth-graders in schools throughout the United States, many of the courses were discontinued or revised.

Public School Awareness groups, started in churches throughout the country, were developed by Citizens for Excellence in Education. In the PSA committee kit there are materials to show how to impact local schools in a positive way. Since 90 percent of church-goers send their children to public schools, it's vital that Christians get involved with how their children are being taught.

Concerned Christians who have organized to debate curricula and classroom practices with school officials often confront accusations that the "religious right" is trying to take over school boards. Alarms are sounded in the media that religious indoctrination will be imposed on the public schools.

Dr. Thomas Sowell, an economist and senior fellow at the Hoover Institute in Stanford, California, said:

> Where have the media been all these years, while the most blatant, deliberate and pervasive indoctrination by the political left has been taking place in public schools all across the country?
>
> Hypothetical dangers from conservative and religious groups attempting to fight back do not begin to compare with the dangers from the enormous apparatus already in place, and continuing to conduct classroom brainwashing, to the detriment of academic education.[18]

Thank you, Dr. Sowell.

Finally, be active. Resolve to pray daily for your children and their schools. Make a friend of your teacher by asking to meet with him or her outside of the usual open-house session or scheduled conference. Stay abreast of what is being taught.

We need to teach our children biblical morality and how to discern for themselves the dangers in anti-Christian teaching. They will either learn New Spirituality or *true* spirituality.

The Bible teaches us that there is an angelic conflict going on around us (Eph. 6:10–18). This battle is intensified when spirit guides and mystical experiences are introduced in the classrooms.

Children can be small but mighty prayer warriors in this spiritual warfare if parents teach them biblical methods. Have them memorize this verse:

> You are of God, little children, and have overcome them, because He who is in you is greater than he who is in the world. (1 John 4:4)

The Heart of Jesus

The value of children seems to have diminished in the minds of many Americans. Parents seem to care less for them, the schools seem to believe it is all right to experiment with their minds, and even churches have lost sight of how precious they are in God's sight. When I began to see the beachhead made by the New Spirituality in our educational system, I was reminded again about what is uppermost in the heart of Jesus. This ought to be in the heart of every one of us.

> About that time the disciples came to Jesus to ask which of them would be greatest in the Kingdom of Heaven!
> Jesus called a small child over to him and set the little fellow down among them, and said, "Unless you turn to God from your sins and become as little children, you will never get into the Kingdom of Heaven. Therefore anyone who humbles himself as this little child, is the greatest in the Kingdom of Heaven. And any of you who welcomes a little child like this because you are mine, is welcoming me and caring for me. But if any of you causes one of these little ones who trusts in me to lose his faith, it would be better for you to have a rock tied to your neck and be thrown into the sea." (Matt. 18:1–6 TLB)

The disciples tried to keep the children away from the Master, but Jesus gave them a lesson in priorities.

> Little children were brought for Jesus to lay his hands on them and pray. But the disciples scolded those who brought them. "Don't bother him," they said.
> But Jesus said, "Let the little children come to me, and don't prevent them. For of such is the Kingdom of Heaven." And he put his hands on their heads and blessed them before he left. (Matt. 19:13–14 TLB)

We only get one chance to bring up our children in the nurture and admonition of the Lord. This is no time to sit on our hands while the enemy is making inroads into our schools and taking our children captive, kidnapping some of them before they are out of kindergarten.

We pray that uppermost in our minds is the realization that the resource of the next generation is in our hands and that God has called us to be concerned about children and young people. Ringing in my ears is the old Sunday school song, "Red and yellow, black and white, they are precious in His sight. Jesus loves the little children of the world."

Can we afford to be less than diligent?

7

CRYSTAL CLEAR

ONE OF THE LEADING EXPONENTS of "psychic gemology" wrote about a certain pastor who had quoted her in a sermon. She said that she was the subject of a forty-five-minute televised Christian service (later rebroadcast on radio) in which the minister gave his audience a "cold, passionless, intellectual talk" on her sins and "the misguidance of the devil in her life." She said he was very uninspiring, when he could have been empowering them with the knowledge of beauty and love. Instead, he warned of the danger of believing that a crystal could be used to attract certair forces that affect our bodies.

The writer continued that she was publicly accused of witchcraft. She said she was going to use her knowledge of white magic to send a message of peace and joy into the invisible world this pastor denied.

When I checked my sermon notes (yes, I am the minister she was writing about), I realized I had used the term *occult practices* in referring to her use of crystal power. I guess I never received the message of her "white magic," because I have had no trouble sleeping at night.

Unfortunately, the lady of the crystals did not realize that my criticism was of her practices, but my desire is for her to turn from alternative spirituality to true spirituality.

This lady sent me a gracious letter saying she had no hopes of changing my mind. However, I pray that somehow the truth of God about the danger in crystal power will penetrate her soul and she will come to know the true power of Jesus Christ in her life.

There are many other kinds of talismans used by alternative spirituality for focusing, centering, meditation, or bio-psychic harmonizing—rocks, feathers, wood, shells, and practically anything "natural." The principles behind crystal power apply to these articles as well.

Rocks in the Mainstream

Crystal power is no longer on the back page of New Age newspapers. It has moved uptown and is shining in the halls of respectability and reflecting through the crystals hanging on the rearview mirrors of automobiles. In full-page ads in *USA Today* and *Parade,* we are enticed to purchase these stones with magical powers. The advertisement copy reads:

> Energy at your fingertips . . . capturing the spirit of well-being and inner harmony. Natural quartz crystal draws the power to you, channeling prisms of light into positive energy. New awareness. New style. The crystal-power ring, set in fascinating sculpture of 22 karat gold coated over solid sterling silver, sparkling with full-cut diamond. Crystal power . . . Priced at just $195. Only from Franklin Mint.[1]

Another offer (just $245) is for a crystal ball.

> For centuries, the crystal ball has been said to foretell the future, to chart one's destiny, and now this wondrous orb of fable and fortune can be yours. Hold it in your hands. Feel its awesome power. Launch yourself on a journey of discovery that will last a lifetime, if you dare. Exclusively from Franklin Mint.[2]

Franklin Mint is the same company that offers collector's plates, special dolls, and porcelain figurines. Now it's also selling power rings and crystal balls. These ads remind us that crystals aren't some weird thing that people talk about when they make fun of New Age religion. They are now front and center. Many major department stores have entire sections where people come to pick out the crystal they need. They are being used by people who think they can help cure anything from heart disease to depression.

The former manager of a downtown San Diego crystal store said, "You can buy crystals for one dollar or several thousand dollars. People these days are more interested than ever in spiritual growth. Crystals are a tremendous tool to go inside and find our connection with that perfect, clear part of ourselves."

The pet-rock fad of the early seventies has been updated, spiritualized, and made trendy. Even comic strips like *Peanuts* show Peppermint Patty gripping a crystal for better grades. In the television movie *The Right to Die*, Raquel Welch, who portrayed a character bedridden from Lou Gehrig's disease, has a crystal wrapped in her palm only minutes before she dies.

A Manhattan businessman has a morning ritual. He drops a small crystal into his pocket to enhance his concentration and aid him in contract negotiations.

Herb Alpert of Tijuana Brass fame tells why he bought a 750-pound slab of quartz in a New York crystal shop. "When I walked into the shop, I could not take my eyes off of it. It makes me feel good to be around it. Since it's from *Him*, you can't not like it."[3]

Those who can't find room in their homes for a gigantic rock can wear their crystals on their fingers, in body pouches, or even drop them in their toilet tanks. The owner of a Manhattan gift shop suggests grinding crystals into powder and mixing it with water to create a drinkable "gem and tonic." He says the crystal sends its vibes through the water, which then charges up the person drinking it.

The most popular use of crystals is to hang them from the rearview mirrors in cars for "traveling mercies." Some crystal-power believers bathe and sleep with crystals; some hang them from the ceilings of their homes or lie silently on their backs with crystals strategically placed on parts of their bodies.

Most crystal users believe the crystal has to be programmed before it can really work for them. One formula for programming is this: First, "clear" the stone by washing it in ocean water or plain saltwater. Then leave it outside for at least twenty-four hours so the rays of the sun and moon may penetrate it. A quicker, high-tech method is to pass an audio-cassette eraser over each side of the crystal for a half a minute. Once you have cleared your crystal, you are now ready to program it.

One method of programming is to hold the crystal in both hands and blow on it while making a wish. No wonder one writer said we ought to call this whole process, *The Saga of the Lost Marbles!*

Skeptics may laugh at the idea of power in crystals, but what about the power of thought? The psalmist said, "Both the inward thought and the heart of man are deep" (Ps. 64:6). Serious practitioners of crystal power claim that various gems have the ability to "soothe our souls and heal our bodies." However, the crystal itself is not the medication that brings about the cure. As Brett Bravo, one of the leading crystal therapists, says, "The cure is centered within the mind of the client, not within the crystal."[4]

The Power of Thought

People who believe in crystals may believe in Jesus Christ but define Him as an "ascended Master," or as "the manifestation of divinity in all of us." Others may be novice Christians who sincerely love the right Jesus but don't understand why crystal practices are contrary to the Bible.

In this rather strange and growing phenomenon, devotees are discovering their thoughts are being taken captive by what they believe are the psychic qualities and healing factors of everything from agates to turquoise.

In the back room of a small store at a crystal-power workshop, five women are seeking to "tap in." One of them says, "Can you feel the energy?"

"I don't know. Can you?"

"Oh, yes," she says. "I feel good every time I wear this necklace. When I take it off, I don't feel the same."

A younger woman, in preparation for a court case later that day, has the workshop leader fill in an entire sheet of notebook paper with a list of rocks she thinks she'll need. Some stones are for traveling mercies while in flight, others for nerves of steel when she takes the stand. Some she will sell to friends to spread the faith and also make a profit.

Choosing a crystal is like choosing a dress or a suit. People have certain styles and colors that are best for them. Don't spend your money on a blue sapphire if you get the best vibrations from a topaz. Crystal healer Brett Bravo says:

> I believe that each person has a superconscious knowing of which crystal is best for them. If one of my clients can have access to view and touch a sample of each of the crystals I use, most choose perfectly for themselves.
>
> I suggest the crystal chosen be kept on the body at all times, worn preferably at the heart chakra on a long chain or at the throat chakra. "Chakra" is the word that is used to designate the power centers of the body by Hindu yogis and others.[5]

There's the Hindu influence again.

I am curious about why it is, if diamonds are a girl's best friend, that every woman didn't choose the diamond as her crystal!

At workshops all over the country, people are learning how they can harness the power of crystals to change their lives. With so many interrelating alternative spirituality practices, it's not surprising that meditation would be involved, even the repetition of certain chants as in the Hindu prayers or mantras.

If you have a particular attraction to pearls, for instance, you may discover certain healing secrets and psychic strengths from this gem. After a lengthy explanation on the chemical composition and the history of pearls, here is what the pearl-wearer could expect:

> If you are ready to allow the Cosmic Current to flow through you as it is meant to do and feel strongly attracted to Pearls, they will aid you. Born in the soothing sea, they continually carry that vibration. Use them to:

1. Smooth over an irritation
2. Increase perfect contemplation
3. Soothe the stomach

    Now . . . here is what you are to do with your pearl:
Place the Pearl(s) against the . . .
    SOLAR PLEXUS (near waist): Cover with palm, re-
peat seven times . . . "These Pearls are vibrating to
smooth over this irritation in my life."
    HEART: Cover with palm, repeat seven times . . .
"These Pearls are vibrating to increase my perfect contemplation."
    FOREHEAD ("third eye"): Cover with palm, repeat
seven times . . . "These Pearls are vibrating to soothe my
judgment center."[6]

Please don't try it. You would be better off with an antacid
tablet and a hot bubblebath.

Why Do Good People Get Bad Vibrations?

Everything in the spiritual realm, according to most New
Spirituality beliefs, is supposed to operate according to exact scientific law. Spiritual energy or healing energy is thought to transmit
at different, definite, and very high vibration levels or frequencies.
    Crystal-power practitioners believe if you put the right crystal
next to your body, it will catch the right frequency to harmonize
you with the essence of the whole. They assume that we have
problems in our lives because the whole is "the one" and until we
are in harmony with "the one" we cannot have peace. So, if you're
having problems at home, difficulties with finances, or can't
sleep at night, you have not yet come into harmonic convergence
with "the one," or "the essence." The only way you can do that
is to change the harmonic frequencies in your life.
    People spend hundreds of thousands of dollars to get the
right crystal with hope that a little rock can change their lives.

Positive or Negative Forces

Alternative spirituality crystal power has no basis in scientific
fact. Tapping or squeezing a crystal produces a very weak charge.

The compression forces the negative and positive ions together, creating a tiny current that flows in one direction. When the pressure is released, the ions return to their original position, giving off a charge flowing in the opposite direction. From the simple quartz-crystal radios that some of us assembled as kids to crystal-controlled frequencies, computers, watches, and lasers, crystals are very important. To move from this scientific fact to the idea that a crystal could respond to the electrical field of a human being and change or enhance his or her distorted spiritual "harmonic field," is outlandish.

I know some people I would categorize as "super-charged," but they didn't use crystals to attain that state! Furthermore, no one I read or heard about stands and squeezes and releases the crystal all the time they're using it. To suggest that a crystal could help you tap into past lives and future events is a scientific absurdity.

Anthony R. Kamptf, curator of minerals and gems at the Los Angeles County Museum of Natural History, said, "With people assigning metaphysical properties to certain minerals, it's shades of the dark ages when there was a certain amount of mysticism associated with minerals. I see a lot of people who are becoming very enamored with certain minerals to which they are assigning these properties, which in scientific terms the minerals don't have."[7]

One geologist said, "It's as close to poppycock as you can get."

Crystals can become objects of demonic influence, just as destructive to mind and soul as magic charms or other occultic articles believed to possess supernatural power for either good or evil use. They become vehicles for spirits to work through, much like divining rods, Ouija boards, or tarot cards. The devil doesn't care whether there is anything inherent in the object at all; if he can get you to put your trust in that object; he can use it as a way to establish a beachhead in your life.

Crystal Power versus Bible Power

When parapsychologist Brett Bravo was interviewed on the Sally Jessy Raphael show in Macon, Georgia, there were reported

to be thirty-five hundred Bible Belt southerners in the audience.
Bravo said:

> I was happy for my Christian background, because I do re-
> member some verses from the Bible and I have done a lot
> of research at the Vatican as well as libraries all over the
> world. I know that there's a tremendous amount of infor-
> mation about the crystals in the Bible and that equally large
> amounts of information have been taken out. I was able to
> tell the audience that if they believed the Bible strictly on
> faith, why would they eliminate the crystal information? It
> comes from the very same book.[8]

Bravo explained to Raphael's predominantly Christian audience that in Exodus (28:15–30), Aaron, the first high priest
of Israel, wore a religious breastplate that had twelve enormous
gems, each inscribed with the name of one of the twelve tribes
of Israel. She said that each gem had mysterious powers that
could be used by the priests in divining matters of law, religion,
war, and healing. She said, "I find it exciting and in many ways
plausible to speculate that this may actually have been a highly
technical computer or inter-galactic communication device."[9]

She says that her own son, a born-again Christian, is concerned about her healing crystal work.

There is no place in the Bible text that says those stones on
Aaron's breastplate carried magical powers. The New Spirituality tries to make the Bible say what the movement wants it to
say, whether or not it says it. The truth is, there are many warnings about worshiping the powers of inanimate objects.

The Tale of the Bronze Snake

Thousands of years ago, the Israelites were wandering in
the desert, tediously making their way from Egypt to the Promised Land. Imagine two million people traveling together for
forty years! Even with the best of leadership and the assurance
that God would provide, it doesn't take much to picture the
grumbling and rebellion in the camps. In the book of Numbers, the story is told about a fierce plague that was sent upon

them; people were being bitten by deadly, poisonous snakes. The people begged Moses to pray that the Lord would take the snakes away.

The Lord told Moses to make a bronze serpent and put it on a pole so that if the people who were bitten looked at it, they would be healed immediately (see Num. 21:4–8). You can imagine how excited everyone in Israel was over the cures that happened because of a metal snake. Moses kept it and placed it among the important possessions of God's people. For a long time in the history of Israel, that bronze serpent was revered, but not worshiped.

Now let's fast-forward a few centuries until we come to the reign of Hezekiah, who was a good king in Israel. The Bible says that Hezekiah destroyed the places where pagan religious ceremonies had been held and got rid of all the cultic objects. This included the bronze serpent Moses had made in the wilderness centuries before. Hezekiah took that old snake, crushed it, and threw it away because the people had turned it from a reminder of God's blessing into an idol of worship (see 2 Kings 18:1–3).

Beauty Is As Beauty Does

Is there any spiritual significance in crystals? No! God made them, and there's no reason why we can't enjoy all the beautiful gems God has made. But if a crystal or any other gemstone is anything other than a beautiful ornament or piece of jewelry, get rid of it. Scripture does not allow for an idea of psychic energy pervading the universe, but it does support the view that demonic energy can be disguised as psychic energy. When people associate crystals with an occult understanding of the universe or look to them for healing or other desired ends, they are opening up a door with their free wills to demonic intrusion and deception. It may be a door they can never close.

Crystals are often bargain quick-fixes for spiritual troubles. I never thought I'd live to see the day when people were so interested in simplistic ways to solve difficult problems. People may spend all their lives getting into trouble and then want someone to resolve it in five minutes. We know, because they call us, and it's not that we don't want to help; but people have to understand that long-term problems do not respond to short-term answers. Long-term problems are usually the result of short-term thinking.

Belief in something like a crystal does two things: It avoids personal responsibility and acts as a substitute for God.

Crystals are powerless unless you give them a place where Satan can use them in your life as a spiritual enticement.

Some people believe that the impact of crystal power has lessened, that its heyday is over. In late 1994, a friend of mine was walking down a street in Orange County and passed a well-known New Age center, but the name had been changed; the image was more upscale. The manager, who held an advanced degree in business, said, "We want to become more part of the mainstream. . . . We are trying to legitimize more." A news article describing one organization, "Learning Light Foundation," was headlined, "Crystal Clear."[10]

Again . . . the image may have changed but not the reality.

I am frightened for my community, my church, and my nation. We are fighting on so many fronts against the New Spirituality that we need to appropriate the strength of the Lord at every turn. I recently received a copy of *The Message,* the New Testament in contemporary English, and found that its translation of the words Paul wrote to Timothy, his son in the faith, spoke to my heart.

> I can't impress this on you too strongly. God is looking over your shoulder. Christ himself is the Judge, with the final say on everyone, living and dead. He is about to break into the open with his rule, so proclaim the Message with intensity; keep on your watch. Challenge, warn, and urge your people. Don't ever quit. Just keep it simple.
>
> You're going to find that there will be times when people will have no stomach for solid teaching, but will fill up on spiritual junk food—catchy opinions that tickle their fancy. They'll turn their backs on truth and chase mirages. *But you—keep your eye on what you're doing; accept the hard times along with the good; keep the Message alive; do a thorough job as God's servant.*[11]

That is good news!

The crystal craze may have peaked, and yet crystals will remain an integral part of the New Spirituality. Like any fad, it explodes and fizzles, but the embers continue to glow.

Crystal healers may work in back rooms, but a new breed of healers has moved into front offices on Main Street. We have appointments with some of them in the next chapter.

8

NEW GODS IN THE WAITING ROOM

IN HIGH SCHOOL AND COLLEGE I played basketball and football, and with our kids involved in sports, I have tried to keep up my athletic activities. However, old back injuries have frequently plagued me, so periodically I've gone to chiropractors. I'll never forget the day I went to one complaining about some problems I had, and he asked me to hold a capsule of some sort in one hand and hold my other arm out at my side. Then he started to push down on my arm. "What's this all about?" I asked, wondering how this would help my back.

He replied that he was doing muscle-reflex testing, which is something I had never heard about. He explained to me that the energy emanating from herbs and vitamins in capsules, even sometimes from thoughts you have, somehow changes the balance or imbalance in your body energy.

The whole procedure puzzled me until years later when I began to learn more about alternative medical practices; these practices often have a spiritual foundation under the umbrella of what is now called holistic medicine.[1]

Incidentally, the process he used is called *applied kinesiology*, a practice I will describe later. His treatment did nothing to help my back problems.

Healthcare Under Assault

A generation ago the picture of the kindly doctor with his little black bag standing at the bedside of a sick child was a comforting sight on the American scene. Norman Rockwell immortalized him on the cover of the *Saturday Evening Post,* and Robert Young made him a household word on the television series *Marcus Welby, M.D.* How the picture has changed! Until recently the successes of the modern medical system have been indisputable. But now the world of physicians, hospitals, and technologists is under attack. In an era of litigation-happy clients, doctors are more stressed than ever. One doctor wrote:

> Most of these attack the way the system does (or does not) deliver the goods: it is seen as too expensive, unfair to the poor, sexist, racist, drug-pushing, time-consuming, and generally hazardous to one's health. While perusing the shelves of the public library one may encounter titles which would cause Marcus Welby to bury his stethoscope: *Don't Get Sick in America* by Daniel Schorr, *The Medical Offenders* by Howard and Martha Lewis . . . to name a few.[2]

When someone is suffering, he or she may do anything to find a cure. An alternative to doctors' prescriptions has been the holistic health movement, which presents itself as promoting "natural" healing and physically "noninvasive" procedures. According to one of its own advocates, it is experiencing a sense of well-being through the proper balance and understanding of body, mind, and spirit.

Holistic health is a leading player in the New Spirituality. In our desire to live longer, be healthier, and look better, we are prone to fall for the claims of someone who offers a new way of healing using unconventional means. We certainly have no quarrel with any health practice with proven safety and effectiveness, but we are concerned about the promotion of methods that have not been proven or are questionable on either physical or spiritual principles.

When I spoke on the subject of holistic medicine on my radio program, "Turning Point," I heard from a lady who said that I gave so many disclaimers before I spoke that she wondered if I really believed what I said. She didn't understand how my strong convictions *compel* me to make careful disclaimers. I am convinced that the New Spirituality emphasis that has crept into alternative health and medicine is a dangerous, insidious poison that is spiritually toxic to those who participate in it. That is why it is so important to distinguish between legitimate health practices and alternative spirituality prescriptions.

Here are my important disclaimers: *Not everyone who espouses the things I'm going to write about should be labeled New Spiritualist or even New Age. In fact, not all that I write about could be called wrong or sinful.* However, I am deeply concerned that many Christians are undergoing treatment from holistic health proponents without questioning the spiritual aspects of their practices.

One doctor wrote, "There are few doubts about the demonic nature of black magic, Satanism, and psychic healing. But the kingdom of darkness has a twilight zone which is equally dangerous. Many a patient has already become hopelessly lost by turning to obscure methods in his quest for healing."[3]

What we hope to do in this chapter is to shed some light on that twilight zone so we won't lose our way in the halls of alternative health and healing.

Out of the Back Room, into the Front Office

As I began reading, talking to people about their experiences, and trying to discern the underlying spiritual meanings in holistic medicine and its offshoots, certain phrases and words seemed to constantly surface. *Body, mind, spirit. Energy healing. Natural substances. Wellness.* All of these sound so right, so needed for the health of our bodies . . . so why do we question them?

One hot summer afternoon, I was wading through a pile of books, newspaper articles, and letters from radio listeners about holistic health. My energy was at a low ebb, and I was contemplating a tall glass of iced tea when my secretary buzzed and said that a member of my church wanted to give me something to help with my research. He came in and handed me an invitation he had received to an Energy Mastery Seminar. I was interested in what the doctor who was conducting the seminar had to say since I could have used some energy right then.

> Advanced Energy Healing is not just about healing and it's not just about energy. It's about the understanding of the nature of this world, the true nature of this reality. . . .
> We are able to uplift the world, and most importantly, we are able to heal the world: its people, animals, plants, minerals, and all kingdoms of nature.

This information was sent out to many offices around the country, encouraging people to come to a two-day seminar and learn how to manipulate the energy within. The medical doctor conducting these seminars devotes all of his time to teaching worldwide. When I looked at the long list of doctors and nurses who were trainers in "Energy Healing," I noticed that two of them were nurses in my hometown.

I got my iced tea, grabbed a pen and a yellow tablet, and began to jot notes on these new spiritual threats right in my own neighborhood. I was determined to shed the light of God's Word on the darkness of this spiritual quackery.

Three of the most influential men promoting a New Spirituality in medical practices are Dr. Deepak Chopra, Dr. Bernie Siegel, and reporter and journalist Bill Moyers.

Dr. Chopra became a luminary in medical circles when his book *Ageless Body, Timeless Mind* hit the bestseller list and stayed there for many weeks. His initial core of followers came from the Transcendental Meditation movement since he was a former associate of the Maraharishi Mahesh Yogi, but his proponents grew as alternative health practices became more accepted. He grabbed my attention when he became the head of Sharp HealthCare's Center for Mind-Body Medicine, a prestigious hospital near my home. Under Chopra's leadership, the center promotes a system of ancient Indian healing principles known as Ayurveda. In an interview, Chopra explained that "Ayurvedic medicine is a six-thousand-year-old holistic system of healing and prolonging life. . . . Ayurveda's pursuit was essentially a spiritual one, focusing not so much with disease as with the experience of health." He said that the goal of Ayurveda was "to confront and discover the spirit as real force. Mysterious, abstract, incomprehensible, but experiential."[4]

Chopra's ideas about the aging process are intriguing, and many of them, such as good nutrition and exercise, are valid. However, basic Hindu ideas permeate his practices. When a Christian doctor in our congregation objected to our local hospital having Chopra head the Center for Mind-Body Medicine, he received an answer that strongly disagreed with him. He was told that mind-body medicine is not associated with any religion.

If that is true, why, may I ask, does Dr. Chopra say it uses the ancient Hindu healing principles known as Ayurveda? Chopra says Ayurveda has a "deeper spiritual basis." In his book he describes it this way:

> According to Ayurveda, the life energy, or Prana, is channeled throughout our bodies by a "wind" known as *Vata*. Vata is one of the three metabolic principles (*doshas*) that give form to every living thing, be it a mosquito, an elephant, a human being, a planet, a star, or the entire cosmos.[5]

It seems to me that if I have the same "life energy" as a mosquito or an elephant, that is a clear assumption of Hindu pantheism. How, then, can it be said that Chopra's practices are "not religious?"

The *Los Angeles Times* reported, "A widely quoted study in the *New England Journal of Medicine* suggests that a third of Americans spend $14 billion a year on alternative medical methods. Eighty percent of those continue to see their regular doctors, a strategy that fits with how the Sharp institute sees ayurveda blending with conventional treatment."[6]

Incidentally, just to clarify the definition of "alternative medicine," the National Institute of Health says "Alternative medicine is any method that is not taught in medical schools, not covered by insurance, and not considered to have sufficient documentation in the United States to prove its safety and effectiveness."[7]

Chopra said he is confident that medical traditionalists have little choice regarding the inescapable paradigm shift (a phrase frequently repeated in New Spiritualist jargon) to what has become a twenty-billion-dollar industry. "It shall be forced upon them," he says resolutely.[8]

Part of the enormous success of his bestseller, *Ageless Body, Timeless Mind,* Chopra attributes to book-buying baby boomers, who are now pushing fifty. It was facetiously reported that, "They teem to his lectures by the Volvo-load."[9]

Another leading exponent of alternative medicine is Dr. Bernie Siegel, author of *Love, Medicine, and Miracles.* He said, "Feeling good about life helps us physically." I could endorse that, but as I read farther in his book, I realized that this much-quoted doctor has his very own spirit guide. He said he was meditating one day when George came into his life, "a bearded, long-haired young man wearing an immaculate flowing white gown and a skullcap. . . . I suppose you may call George a 'meditatively released insight from my unconscious,' or some such, if you must have an intellectual label for him. All I know is that he has been my invaluable companion ever since his first appearance. My life is much easier now, because he does the hard work. . . George also helped me see things about medicine that I'd missed before."[10]

Do mainstream writers accept Siegel's views? Watch for his name in popular magazines and periodicals. You'll even find him quoted when you're flying on business or vacation. In the August 1990 issue of *USAir Magazine,* the writer for the health section wrote a glowing account of "healing from within" and endorsed Siegel's views and the practice of self-healing. If it takes a spirit guide by the name of George to direct the medical advice of our physicians, I believe we're all in trouble.

One of the most seductive and provocative presentations of the New Spirituality in medicine has been made by the well-known reporter Bill Moyers. The word *seductive* is used because Moyers has had a reputation as a respected journalist. He was a Southern Baptist, having graduated from conservative Southwestern Theological Seminary, but he has changed his membership to the liberal United Church of Christ and has taken a significant turn to the religious left, embracing the ideology of alternative medicine.

Moyers had a five-part series on PBS in October 1993, entitled "Healing and the Mind"; he also wrote a companion book with the same name. He presents himself as an investigative journalist so we feel safe with his views, but he fails to provide any scientific refutation for many of the Eastern beliefs and practices in his reports.

I listened to the tape transcripts of Moyers's visit to China and his introduction to the products of Chinese medicine, particularly what he called the "mystery of Ch'i," healing methods with herbs, needles, massage, and meditation. I found that his interviews with Chinese doctors were fascinating, but I was disturbed by the underlying beliefs in mind-body healing.

In Moyers's tapes I heard about the bio-energy, the life force of Chinese medicine. He said that to the Chinese, the body is based on energy, which is said to flow through all living organisms.

Chinese medicine is really the child of their religion, with the same ingredients as the Tao, yin and yang, the universal energy Ch'i, and five therapies.[11]

Many Americans have probably come across some forms of Chinese medicine without realizing it—acupuncture and acupressure, for instance. The philosophical underpinnings of acupuncture are in Taoism, an ancient Chinese religion. Taoism, unlike biblical teaching, does not distinguish between good and evil, God and Satan. Such teaching is called *monism,* and it is a basic assumption in all Eastern religions as well as in modern holistic therapies. "Chinese medicine understands man as one in body and spirit, a complete unit, finding its ultimate harmony only in Tao."[12]

Why am I concerned? Here's what a Christian physician says:

People who know nothing of ancient Chinese religion will tell you how energy flows through their bodies in invisible channels. Individuals who would never dream of calling themselves Taoists are concerned about whether they have an imbalance of yin and yang. In essence, Chinese medicine is providing a way for people (including many Christians who accept Scripture as authoritative) to act like

mystics without realizing it and perhaps to become mystics
. . . the transformation of thinking comes along with
simple techniques for achieving some other purpose, such
as relaxation or feeling more energetic.[13]

A writer for the *New Age Journal* watched the Moyers PBS
program and said it would help viewers gain a wider apprecia-
tion of ideas still finding their way into the mainstream. I believe
that writer was wrong . . . it is in the mainstream *now*.

Under the Umbrella of Holistic Practices

It's true that many people are growing tired of some of the
drugs, surgery, and other conventional ways of treatment. They
are looking for disease-preventative healthy living. However, we
need to be careful and not fall for the questionable claims and
practices associated with some forms of alternative healthcare.
Here are a few:

Homeopathy is based on the principle of "like cures like." In
other words, the same substance causing symptoms in a healthy
person will cure those symptoms in a sick person. It claims to work
by correcting an imbalance or problem in the body's "vital force"
or life-energy that is currently making the person ill, or will later
manifest itself as disease. The homeopathic diagnosis and treatment of illness were developed by a medical rebel and mystic,
Samuel Hahnemann, in the early 1800s; today there are several
thousand homeopaths who treat many satisfied customers. But,
again, beware. Here is one explanation of how homeopathy can cure:

> Man is a spiritual being and only the spirit can heal the
> body. Illness only exists because the spirit of Man considers
> that illness can exist. By presenting to the spirit (or vital
> force) the correct medicine in the correct dose for the cor-
> rect period of time, the spirit changes its considerations and
> the illness is gone.[14]

When the homeopathic practitioners claim they work upon
the "vital force," we should be forewarned that occult practices
can lie beneath the surface.

Herbal Remedies, Natural or Supernatural?

Buried under the dust of ancient civilizations are voluminous books about healing herbs. In the Bible, King Hezekiah was given a poultice of figs for a painful boil, and he recovered (see 2 Kings 20:7).

Today herbs are used to treat cancer, cardiovascular diseases, hypertension, glaucoma, the digestive system, and other diseases. Most of us have taken herbal remedies in one form or another. I had honestly thought that if it's natural, it can't hurt you. However, I have learned that herbs can contain potent chemicals, some of which are toxic. A CNN special on *Herbs: Myth or Medicine?* reported that there are at least thirty herbs on the market that are considered by medical experts as potentially harmful. On the other hand, there are many herbs, such as chamomile, garlic, peppermint, and flax seed, that are known to have healing properties.

My educational degrees are not in medicine but in theology. However, if herbal medicine and natural remedies of the health-food faddists contain a spiritual agenda, that is my field. At the Whole Life Expo held in San Diego in 1993, the list of lectures with spiritualist and occultic overtones was extensive. "Eating nutrient-dense superfoods empowers your body, mind, and spirit!" "Learn how to reach higher levels of gratification: physically, spiritually, and sensually, through the erotic usage of foods and aphrodisiacs."

Be alert to the fact that the search for a new diet may lead you to a new world-view.

Acupuncture and acupressure make use of the belief that "energy flow" can be redirected to balance healing energies by inserting needles (acupuncture) or by applying pressure (acupressure) to specific points on the body.

Based on the occultic religion of Taoism, the claims of these practices are centered upon the ability to simulate the flow of cosmic life-energy through alleged invisible channels or "meridians" in the body. "When the body organs or systems are supposedly deficient in a proper supply of *ki* (Japanese) or *C'hi* (Chinese) energy, imbalance is allegedly produced, resulting in disease. Restoring the flow of psychic energy through the meridians is believed to revitalize the body organs and systems, thereby curing illness and maintaining health."[15]

That explanation leaves a lot of unanswered questions, but most people want to know the bottom line. Does it work? Certainly many people attest to the fact that their migraine headaches responded to acupressure when all else failed or the pain in their necks evaporated when no drugstore pill worked. The rich and famous have touted its virtues:

> Actress Jaclyn Smith had whiplash. James Garner had pain in his knee. Robert Wagner wanted to quit smoking. Merv Griffin was exhausted. What did they do? Each went to see Zion Yu, Hollywood's leading acupuncturist. Yu jokes he has needled more people than Don Rickles and Rona Barrett combined.[16]

It is not just the celebrity circuit that is turned on to acupuncture. It has become a respectable research topic in Western universities and medical centers. However, classical acupuncture carries its metaphysical baggage, involving the practice of ancient pagan medicine tied to Taoism, and is deliberately or inadvertently involved with psychic healing.

Applied Kinesiology is a common type of practice that many Christians find themselves exposed to through chiropractors and nutritional counselors. (This is how I was treated years ago.) There is a difference between the scientific discipline of formal kinesiology and the applied kinesiology originating from the Eastern religious concept of energy.

At Christian Heritage College, we teach the scientific discipline of kinesiology as part of the physical education program. This is the study of principles, mechanics, and anatomy in relationship to the science of human muscular movement. It is frequently used in the study of physical education and physical therapy.

Applied kinesiology originated with George Goodheart, a chiropractor who combined the concept of "innate intelligence" with the Eastern religious concept of energy and the idea that muscles reflect the condition of each of the various body organs via the Ch'i meridians. The "innate intelligence" is described as spiritual intelligence that runs the body and is connected to the universal intelligence through the nervous system.

Kinesiologists claim the energy emanating from herb and vitamin capsules or even thoughts somehow balance (or unbalance) the body energy. For instance, in demonstrating how muscle-response testing works, a kinesiologist focused on a thought about a client, then checked the client's fingers for the response. The practitioner's positive thought led to "strength" in the client, thus "validating" that procedure.

After reading about kinesiology, I began to feel a little unbalanced myself! The power to alter someone else's "energy field" is not biblical Christianity but occultism or quackery, no matter how nice the practitioner is.

Unfortunately, some Christian writers have painted the entire chiropractic profession with New Spirituality colors, which is unfair. The Christian Chiropractors Association sent me its policy statement in which the organization takes a stance on New Age healing.

They say, "In order that we might have clear discernment of Satan's deceptive methods, we adopt the following guidelines in identifying New Age healing: Healing which applies occult energies, forces, chi, yin, yang, magnetic healing, life essence, cosmic consciousness, psychic diagnosis, astrology, channeling, etc. . . . The scriptures clearly teach against this practice."[17]

The Rev. Roland Murphy, executive director of the Christian Chiropractors Association, said, "We encourage Christian patients who are discerning to ask a doctor, 'What is your belief system? Do you believe in creationism, pantheism, or Christianity?'"[18]

We must be willing to examine those practices we do not understand while maintaining discernment about therapies that support a world-view that is antagonistic to Scripture.

Iridology is the study of the iris of the eye. Don't look for romance here. This is not the soul-searching look of someone in love. It is a method by which proponents believe they can detect illness or weakness in specific body tissues and, based on that assessment, use diet and herbs for treatment. They also believe they can assess mental, sexual, and emotional problems through the iris-body connection.

Although iridology may not fall into the category of New Spirituality, it is true that some of its proponents frequently use Scripture to support their views, including Matthew 6:22–23: "The lamp of the body is the eye. If therefore your eye is good, your whole body will be full of light. But if your eye is bad, your whole body will be full of darkness." This is speaking of spiritual illness, not any bodily manifestation. In addition to misuse of Scripture, the claims of iridologists have not been substantiated by years of documented scientific research.

In Escondido, California, Bernard Jensen, who is not a medical doctor, is known as the father of modern iridology. According to an interview on CNN in August 1993, Jensen uses his practice, not only to detect disease conditions, but also to recommend nutritional therapy using herbal products. We played the videotape of this interview at our church and found it was a real eye-opener. (No pun intended.) The reporter consulted five iridologists in individual sessions and each time had more bad news. He was told he had problems with his stomach, colon, and back, and had parasites. The diagnoses were different and contradicted each other. After these revelations, he needed another opinion, so he went to see his own doctor.

"Well, as you know, last week we gave you a thorough examination. I'm delighted to tell you that everything came out remarkably healthy. In fact, it would have been impossible for anyone who had all those other problems to come into my office walking."

Thanks to a clean bill of health that the reporter got from his doctor, he didn't waste several hundred dollars on the particular herbal products recommended by the iridologists. But, for those with real health problems, the stakes are higher. People could be taking herbs pitched by the herbal distributors instead of treatments prescribed by medical professionals.

Buyer Beware

When I see the number of ideas being touted in holistic medicine, it is dizzying. Many of them are old precepts brought up to date, polished, and encased in a new package. The diagnostic and therapeutic regimes being sold are multiplying as medical costs skyrocket. A few of the common ones are: aromatherapy, polarity therapy, Touch for Health, reflexology, aura reading, therapeutic touch, Bach flower remedies, and, of course, the ones we've mentioned. How do we evaluate the validity of a treatment or practice from a spiritual, as well as rational, view? Do we need to be like those who say all of our favorite foods and drinks are carcinogenic? Or do we blindly accept advice if it comes from a Christian or someone whose educational credentials are impressive?

Who's right? Who's wrong? Where do I find the guidelines to make a decision when someone in my family is ill or I am suffering? A world-view based upon God's view is the answer.

1. *Research the origins of a practice.* Does it have its roots in Hinduism, Taoism, or other religions and beliefs? Is it pantheistic in its view? Does it have occultic tones?

The Bible says, "Test all things; hold fast what is good. Abstain from every form of evil" (1 Thess. 5:21–22).

2. *Does the practice really work?* Stories and testimonies are interesting, but they do not prove anything by themselves. I sometimes hear people say that the best thing you can do when you are trying to win someone to Christ is to tell them your story. Who am I to say that my story is any better than yours, if it is not based upon objective evidence and fact? Do you know why I know I am a Christian? Not because Jesus makes me feel better or not because I talked to Him this morning, as important as that is. I know I am a Christian because I have examined the evidence of the historical person of Jesus Christ and I know for a fact that He went to the cross and that He came out victorious over death. There is more evidence for that than there is that Abraham Lincoln ever lived. I believe that with all of my heart because I have examined the evidence. If we can do that with our faith, we can do that with our medical alternatives. "Let no one deceive you by any means" (2 Thess. 2:3a).

3. *If it works, is it right?* Some holistic practices actually work; that is, they bring about desired results. In fact, the healing may be quite dramatic. But is the practice based on accurate physiology? Are there reputable scientific studies that support

or disprove the therapy? Is the practice accepted by the science and health community as valid?

If alternative medical practices do result in cures or physical improvements, there may be several explanations. The patient may have regained health with or without the particular therapy; the cure may be the result of a placebo effect (this is a term to define a medication that is prescribed only to please the patient but contains no actual health-related ingredients); the healers, with their remedies and therapies, may trigger the actual, though not yet fully understood effect; suggestion or hypnosis may somehow be involved in the healing; the patient is healed through the direct influence of demonic powers.

It may work, but it may not be right, either spiritually or physically.

"But, Pastor Jeremiah, my therapist (or doctor) is a Christian. He was recommended by someone right here in the church."

I would rather place my trust in a Christian doctor, but even he or she could be unwittingly involved in New Spiritualist thinking. The endorsement of a therapist or therapy by a celebrity, even a renowned evangelical pastor, is no guarantee of legitimacy. We need to do our homework and ask questions as if our lives depended upon it.

Our Attitude, Our Health

Someone has said that attitude is everything. The Bible agrees with the New Spiritualist idea that one's mental attitude affects health. Proverbs 3:7–8 says, "Do not be wise in your own eyes; fear the LORD and depart from evil. It will be health to your flesh, and strength to your bones."

When one of my friends was severely ill in the hospital, his daughter brought him Bible verses and tacked them on the bulletin board where he could see them every day.

He said, "You know, all the medicine in the world couldn't have done what the Word of God did for me. Those verses were my strength when I didn't have any of my own."

Here are two of those verses:

And He said to me, "My grace is sufficient for you, for My strength is made perfect in weakness." Therefore most gladly I will rather boast in my infirmities, that the power of Christ may rest upon me. (2 Cor. 12:9)

> Bless the LORD, O my soul,
> And forget not all His benefits:
> Who forgives all your iniquities,
> Who heals all your diseases,
> Who redeems your life from destruction,
> Who crowns you with lovingkindness and
>   tender mercies,
> Who satisfies your mouth with good things,
> So that your youth is renewed like the eagle's.
>   (Ps. 103:2–5)

My friend is now recovering from that illness and says, "God's presence has never been more real to me than it was during those weeks in the hospital, and His Word has never been more personal."

For the Christian, one's body, mind, and (Holy) Spirit are sacred trusts.

Or do you not know that your body is the temple of the Holy Spirit who is in you, whom you have from God, and you are not your own? For you were bought at a price; therefore glorify God in your body and in your spirit, which are God's. (1 Cor. 6:19–20)

Prayer to the one God is the most powerful healing method available to the believer. Today, the medical community is acknowledging the effects of prayer on health and healing, something the Bible has taught for four thousand years.

We realize that our personal attitudes, emotions, and lifestyles, as well as self-destructive habits (smoking, overeating, substance abuse) influence our health and well-being. "Physical by-products of long-term anger, anxiety and loneliness may include such diverse problems as headaches, peptic ulcer disease, irritable colon syndrome, and possible cancer."[19]

Even the basic belief of the holistic health movement—integrating body, mind, and spirit—sounds good. However, listen to this statement by the president of the California Academy of Preventive Medicine:

> Holistic Health is a state of being in which a person is integrated in all of his levels of being: body, mind, and spirit. . . . The attainment of this state of integration . . . brings into existence an entirely new person, different from what existed before, and at a new plateau of existence. I submit that this new state of being of an individual is a state of self realization or self actualization or enlightenment.[20]

"Enlightenment" is equated with Eastern mysticism in which psychic or supernatural experiences may occur. Do you think Christians should be involved in any of these practices? Do we want *self*-enlightenment or *God*-enlightenment?

The answers to those questions are a matter of life and death. "Now may the God of peace Himself sanctify you completely; and may your whole spirit, soul, and body be preserved blameless at the coming of our Lord Jesus Christ" (1 Thess. 5:23).

True holistic healing comes from the greatest Healer of all time, Jesus Christ.

9

CORPORATE TAKEOVERS

WHEN *JONATHAN LIVINGSTON SEAGULL,* the intriguing allegory by Richard Bach, flew into the American scene twenty years ago, the young, adventuresome gull set the stage for human flight into another dimension. Instead of the dull, routine life of slogging back and forth to the fishing boats, Jonathan found a route to a more abundant life. He discovered the fresh winds of freedom and creativity through the secrets of self-actualization.

"We can find ourselves as creatures of excellence and intelligence and skill. We can be free! We can learn to fly!"[1]

What a trip that bird had! He was led upward by a couple of bird guides to a flock of glorified gulls. They taught him that life is like a wheel where the consequences of one's deeds follow him through transmigrations or reincarnations. He was instructed in the art of love, and eventually Jonathan became a missionary pilot who returned to convert other misguided gulls to his version of an abundant life.

He was a bird ahead of his time, and he prepared the way for the message that man can soar above his peers if he is empowered by the spirit within himself.

Sounds wonderful, doesn't it? Now let's take Jonathan's mission out of a fanciful piece of fiction and send it to some of our largest United States corporations. Translate the language to include such concepts as employee assessment, stress management, consciousness-raising, self-improvement, and increased productivity, and you have an appealing package that may contain New Spirituality components.

Psychological techniques have been introduced into the business world for the purpose of gaining new insights into personal worth and improving management skills. These are laudable goals, but when the training methods used in some of the seminars and workshops intrude upon one's religious beliefs or undermine Christian principles, the caution sign needs to flash.

Buzzwords Enter the Gates of Corporate America

One of the most respected analysts of American business trends is Peter Drucker. When I was in seminary, I read his book *The Effective Executive* and was impressed by his logical approach to business. In the February 9, 1989, issue of the *Wall Street Journal*, he had some sharp-edged comments about a wave of "pop-psychology hitting American management." He wrote:

> These programs use their own terminology—a mixture of computer jargon and the "self-realization" of the flower children of the '60s. Otherwise, however, they are strikingly similar to earlier psychological fads that have hit U.S. business.
>
> In the late '20s and early '30s, managements became infatuated with auto-hypnosis, exemplified by the wildly popular "mantra" of French guru Dr. Emile Coue: "Every day, in every way, I am getting better and better." Repeated morning, noon and night, it was guaranteed to make a superman out of the worst wimp. In the late '50s and early '60s, we had the "sensitivity training" of "T-groups." Now we have "conscious-raising."

Drucker warned, "Company-ordered psychological seminars are an invasion of privacy not justified by any company need. They are morally indefensible and bitterly resented."

Even when attendance is voluntary, what is a person to do? If your job or promotion is at stake, you do what is "suggested" by your boss.

We asked Professor Drucker, "Are these types of seminars continuing in American businesses? Are they as prevalent as they were in 1989 when you wrote for the *Wall Street Journal?*"

In a reply to our letter, he said, "Of course this type of seminar is continuing—con men never give up. But all of the fads now are 'hard' . . . re-engineering, down-sizing, outsourcing, and so on. In the five-year cycles in which management fads tend to go, we are now in year three of the 'hard' cycle. Wait another two years until the next 'soft' fun gets going. It will."[2]

Here are my disclaimers again: Not all motivational speakers should be painted with the same brush. Zig Ziglar and Charlie "Tremendous" Jones, for example, are popular writers and speakers who combine motivation and humor with Christian principles.

However, many motivational business seminars are founded on the Eastern philosophical view that man is divine and thus the master of his own fate. Their jargon may contain words like: *self-actualization, meditation, transformation, self-talk, positive affirmations, perceived reality.* These are just a few of the buzzwords being heard in business meetings and motivational workshops that are espousing New Spirituality training.

Why do they appeal to men and women in the business world? Tal Brooke, who came full circle from worshiping an Indian guru to belief in Christ, is a knowledgeable spokesman on spiritual counterfeits. He wrote:

> The millions of members of the corporate and business work force comprise a significant captive audience. Why? Because they live in a competitive environment that is full of peer pressure, the need for corporate approval and advancement, as well as one of the deepest human needs, the need for financial security. . . . They have conformed to get where they are, and they will continue to conform to get ahead.[3]

The names of some of these seminars may be changed, just as "New Age" has tried to drop its label, but the basic assumptions and beliefs remain. Some of the names are: Pacific Institute of Seattle (Lou Tice seminars), est, The Forum, Silva Mind Control,

Dianetics, Krone Training, Innovation Associates, Lifespring, Transformational Technologies, and Summit Workshops.

The "transformation" recommended by the founders and leaders of these business seminars has spiritual implications that a non-Christian or new believer may not recognize. The belief that human beings can change themselves by calling upon the power (or god) within or their own infinite human potential is a contradiction of the Christian view. The Bible says man is a sinner and is saved by God's grace alone. Presented in culturally attractive packages, some of these motivational messages may be alternative spirituality in designer clothes.

A Christian mini-seminar was written by Paul to the church at Rome: "And do not be conformed to this world, but be transformed by the renewing of your mind, that you may prove what is that good and acceptable and perfect will of God" (Rom. 12:2).

Contrast the biblical view with that of Anthony Robbins, an "acknowledged expert in the psychology of change," according to the jacket credits on his book *Awakening the Giant Within*. Robbins says we can set up our own "Master System" to take control of our lives and harness the forces that shape our destiny. Robbins and his companies, through Success Systems, Destiny Financial Services, and other far-flung enterprises, bring his attractively packaged and presented ideas to thousands of businesses and individuals. The bottom line is that Robbins provides certain values and principles to create our own *ultimate destiny*. The method of change Robbins promotes is called "Neuro-Linguistic Programming." He says:

> Just after my twenty-first birthday, I was exposed to a series of technologies that could make changes in people's lives with lightning-like speed; simple technologies like Gestalt therapy, and tools of influence like Ericksonian hypnosis and Neuro-Linguistic Programming. When I saw that these tools could really help people create changes in *minutes* that previously took months, years, or decades to achieve, I became an evangelist in my approach to them. I decided to commit all of my resources to mastering these technologies.[4]

One of the great techniques of the human potential leaders is to use Scripture to support their views. Robbins quoted 1 Corinthians 15:51: "Behold, I tell you a mystery: We shall not all sleep, but we shall all be changed—in a moment, in the twinkling of an eye."

The Scripture Robbins quoted refers to the Rapture, a time when Christ will come for all believers before the seven-year Tribulation. This is the pre-Tribulation view, which I hold. (A mystery is a revealed truth that man cannot discern by human wisdom.) Some Christians may identify that verse with the resurrection of all believers at the Second Coming of Christ. However, using that Bible verse as an analogy for "Neuro-Linguistic Programming" is a gross distortion.

Who Opened the Door to the Board Room?

The corporate business world did not introduce these New Age trainings from a vacuum. Even when the craze for these types of seminars has died out, the underlying occult ideology will remain. It's like the world of high fashion where new clothes are introduced each season.

The human potential movement has established a firm beachhead in our society as more and more Americans believe in their own ability to transform themselves and the world. The basic philosophy is faith in man's unlimited capabilities to change himself.

I can already hear some of you saying, "That's right . . . whatever the mind of man can conceive and believe it can achieve." Millions have repeated that phrase from *Think and Grow Rich* by Napoleon Hill, not realizing that the faith expressed is a blind faith in the ability to be one's own god.

As American businessmen and women seek to find ways to become more competitive, efficient, and profitable, they have succumbed to programs that may appeal to emotions rather than reason. Sometimes the dividing line between what is basic management training and what is bunk is hard to pin down.

The history of the business world's involvement in the New Spirituality began when ancient wisdom was repackaged for

modern consumption by people like the Maharishi and his Transcendental Meditation and the late L. Ron Hubbard, founder
of Scientology.

TM lost its credibility and general appeal because of its increasingly foolish claims, its implausible leader, and legal
irregularities. However, there were still many people who believed its claims for the power of meditation while discounting
TM's increasingly weird image.

Into every void a successor must walk. Although he had
never been a TM trainer, one of the most effective inheritors of
the Maharishi's tarnished legacy was Jack Rosenberg. To suit a
new, more exotic image, he changed his name to Werner Erhard.

In 1963, Erhard claimed to have an "enlightenment experience" that prompted him to search for religious/existential
disciplines for permanent enlightenment. "The best from all of
these sources were combined with Erhard's own mystical experiences to produce Erhard Seminars Training (est). During
Erhard's search he tried Scientology, Mind Dynamics, Zen Buddhism, Hinduism, hypnosis, Yoga, Silva Mind Control,
psychocybernetics, Gestalt and encounter therapy and others.
Finally, in 1971, he reached permanent enlightenment by realizing "What is, is, and what isn't, isn't."[5]

Human Potential Trendsetters

Est was probably the biggest of the "consciousness raising"
seminars in the 1970s. Est is a version of Eastern mysticism and
human-potential psychology packaged in a high-pressure group
situation. The stories coming out of the two consecutive week-
end seminars tell of hours upon hours of techniques that served
to break down one's inhibitions, traditions, and moral structure
and insert new patterns and structures. According to a young
businessman who became involved with est, "Soon the trainees
come to think that they have everything they need; they're
totally self-sufficient. Self is god. This process is called enlightenment."[6]

How does someone like Werner Erhard dream up a system
and a philosophy like est? Tal Brooke relates how Erhard made

several trips to India to sit with Swami Muktananda. In fact, "Erhard used to boast that Muktananda hit him with a power touch on the third eye, giving him an enlightenment experience."[7]

He later began to study the emerging human-potential movement, Zen Buddhism, and hypnosis, and took courses from Dale Carnegie, Scientology, and California's Esalen Institute.[8]

The seminars that Erhard started eventually spawned a multimillion-dollar business, attracting thousands of followers. The est trainers of the 1970s were dictatorial and dogmatic toward the trainees. It's hard to imagine that people paid big money to be sequestered in a room, told when and if they could go to the bathroom, deprived of food and sleep, and broken emotionally, all in the name of self-improvement!

Noted "estians" included celebrities like John Denver, Yoko Ono, Joanne Woodward, Cher, Polly Bergen, Norman Lear, Judy Collins, and Diana Ross, plus corporate and professional leaders of such prestigious institutions as MIT, the American Management Association, Harvard Business School, and Stanford Business School, all of whom sat at the feet of Erhard himself.[9]

Just as we have seen, the consistent pattern is that when a group or organization begins to fall into disrepute, it turns the corner and changes its name. In this manner est has had a facelift. Out of est came The Forum, and from that has come a franchise called Trans Technologies. Names have changed, techniques have been made more palatable for the business community to swallow, but the underlying belief system is still the same. Tal Brooke, writing in *Spiritual Counterfeits Project Journal* said:

> The est teaching was that people had total responsibility for creating reality and had to admit that they had created everything in their lives, positive and negative. Now The Forum uses the word "choice." People choose things to happen. They formulate life scripts. The Forum does not have est's guided fantasies preceded by body-relaxation techniques. But people are still encouraged to reveal themselves on the most intimate level in order to be free from the need to protect their images.[10]

Est, etc.

The November 23, 1987, issue of *Fortune* had a feature article on New Age corporate seminars and named three that dominated the human potential movement of the seventies: MSIA (pronounced "Messiah"), John Hanley's Lifespring, and est.

MSIA is the brainchild of John-Roger, who has been selling its courses, Insight I, II, and III, as "intensive growth experiences" for individuals. John-Roger drew a large group of disciples who believed he was the embodiment of a Christlike power called the "Mystic Traveler Consciousness." He claimed that he left the earth after an operation in 1962 and a spiritual entity, "John the Beloved," entered his body. From that time on Roger D. Hinkins became John-Roger.[11]

Fortune magazine reported that MSIA has been boosted by Barbra Streisand, Leigh Taylor-Young, and Arianna Staffinopoulos Huffington, who capped a brilliant social career in London and New York by writing a bestseller and marrying Texas millionaire (and California politician) Michael Huffington. "She promoted MSIA by writing about it and introducing John-Roger to her friends. Philip Lippincott, CEO and president of Scott Paper, was captivated by John-Roger's seminars at the beginning of the eighties and offered them at company expense to all employees."[12]

Employees of companies where these seminars were compulsory or "strongly suggested" have fought back. Many of them have been fired for refusing to attend.

When I was speaking on this subject in 1990, we had some church members who were employed by a large California company. There was a major issue in our community because this company had made it mandatory for these Christian people to go to New Age seminars for motivation. Some of them refused, and I know of at least one person who lost his job because of it. His was certainly not an isolated case.

The *New York Times* reported that the manager of human resources at Firestone Tire and Rubber plant refused to carry out what he described as New Age training offered by the Pacific Institute of Seattle. He said he "adhered to the Christian view that human fate is dependent upon the will of God. In contrast, he said, the course 'focused everything on the self; the self was the center, the source of energy; the self had the ability to deal with any problem in life, you were capable of anything.'"[13]

The number of blatantly New Age business seminars waned as a growing number of workers challenged their employers regarding forced attendance. According to a March 25, 1989, *Los Angeles Times* article, these lawsuits are part of "an emerging backlash against employers who try to boost productivity by requiring workers to take part in so-called human potential seminars, motivational programs designed to change workers' values, attitudes and self esteem."

Many of the complaints were filed with the U.S. Equal Employment Opportunity Commission (EEOC), a government agency that investigates job discrimination claims. The policy notice says, "While there may be some disagreement over whether the training programs themselves are religious, an employee need only demonstrate that participation in the program in some manner conflicts with his/her personal religious beliefs." Those who do this are exempted from attending the program.

Now What?

Once the indoctrination has been done, the infiltration is complete. One day I picked up a sports magazine and discovered that the world of sports fashion has been invaded in force. In the trend for "green cotton and earth-friendly products" companies are saying that "the Eastern philosophies of mind/body/spirit have impacted the way Americans look at their fitness programs." So what do the sportswear manufacturers say? "Virtual reality products could replace drugs," said the director of one sportswear company. "It's all a part of the effort to make gods of everyday persons. The idea of our own spirituality is very much part of all our thinking."[14]

An article in the *Wall Street Journal* drew my immediate attention. There's a place in the "misty foothills of the Blue Ridge Mountains" where people can get away from it all—particularly their bodies. The Monroe Institute is a research outfit devoted to the study and teaching of altered states of consciousness. All you need to do is pay the thirteen-hundred-dollar fee to learn how to have an out-of-body experience.

"Many of the institute's 7,000 graduates hail from the halls of business and industry—even the military. Retired Gen. Albert Stubblebine, former director of the U.S. Army Intelligence and Security Command, confirms that the Army sent personnel to the Institute in the 1980s. At that time, the Army was investigating the potential military applications of psychic phenomenon and 'new age' training techniques."[15]

Out-of-body experiences and altered states of consciousness have no place in business seminars. The new rash of out-of-body and life-after-death reports are experiences that are unbiblical and filled with an occultic view of life.

The inroads of the New Spirituality in American business during the latter part of this century contain danger signs. If we keep absorbing Eastern mysticism in our technologies and motivational seminars, we are going to resemble more of the work ethic of India, which has resulted in one of the lowest standards of living in the world, instead of the work ethic that has made America a great nation.

Why Is It Wrong?

I am a positive thinker. I know who is in charge of my life. I know how everything is going to come out because I've read the end of the Book. But . . . much of what is going on in the seminars that offer "life-changing" experiences is based upon a faulty foundation. For Christians to get involved in compromising the integrity of their faith with humanism is to be involved with a compromised foundation for life. A. W. Tozer once wrote these words:

> It is in this matter of how to deal with man's proud, perverse, sinful nature that we discover two positions within the framework of Christianity. One position is that which leans heavily upon the practice of psychology and psychiatry. There are so-called Christian leaders who insist that

Jesus came into the world to bring about an adjustment to our ego. So there are thousands of referrals as the clergymen shift the problems from the church to the psychiatric couch. On the other hand, thank God the Bible plainly says that Jesus did not come to adjust our egos or end our concern with self-esteem. But Jesus Christ came to bring an end of self, not to educate, tolerate or polish it.[16]

The problem with many of these seminars is that they are built upon the power of the human ego. They are telling you that you can do anything your mind can conceive. That sounds good, and it really appeals to a person who is trying to make it in the business world. However, as believers in Jesus Christ, we know that is not true. We learn that our power often comes in the context of great weakness.

The greatest power I have ever known as a pastor has been in the past few months since I discovered I had lymphoma. My experience has been different from anything I have known in twenty-five years of preaching. In the weakened condition of my body, I have felt the surging power of the Holy Spirit. I told my wife, Donna, that it is almost like listening to someone else preaching. As of the date of this writing, I have not missed one Sunday in the pulpit. I can honestly say that I know what Paul meant when he pleaded with the Lord to take away his thorn in the flesh and the Lord answered, "My grace is sufficient for you, for My strength is made perfect in weakness." Paul then said, "Therefore most gladly I will rather boast in my infirmities, that the power of Christ may rest upon me. . . . *For when I am weak, then I am strong*" (2 Cor. 12:9–10, emphasis mine).

I'm not exactly sure how this would fit into the power seminars.

Moses was not a great speaker, but he obeyed God and led his people out of bondage (see Exod. 4:1–5:27). Daniel was helpless when he was thrown into the lions' den, but he trusted God, and God delivered him (see Dan. 6:1–28). Some of the greatest testimonies I've seen to the power of God have come from people in hospital beds. A positive mental attitude without the Lord is like a bridge without steel supports.

These types of seminars and this ideology have no biblical basis. Scripture teaches us that humanity is fallen and that it cannot achieve reconciliation with God without the saving grace of the Lord Jesus Christ. Salvation cannot come from our works. "For by grace you have been saved through faith, and that not of yourselves: it is the gift of God" (Eph. 2:8).

Setting personal and business goals is not wrong; nor is the desire for personal growth. Some of the greatest Christians I know will acknowledge that it was God's wisdom and power that contributed to their success. What is wrong is the concept that a system of salvation depends on what we can do for ourselves.

C. S. Lewis warned some church leaders that, "Our business is to put what is timeless (the same yesterday, today, and tomorrow) in the particular language of our own age. The bad preacher does exactly the opposite. He takes the ideas of our own age and tricks them out in the traditional language of Christianity."[17]

If we turn on our televisions, we may watch preachers who tell us we can get ahead with positive thinking, we can visualize ourselves as we want to be. They are taking the jargon of marketplace motivation, Christianizing it, and foisting it off on the unwary Christian population.

It isn't that we shouldn't be motivated. It is the basis of that type of motivation that is wrong.

The human potential/New Age/New Spirituality courses do not have a very good record. Let me tell you about one fellow in the Bible who got counsel from someone he shouldn't have.

The Fall of Saul

Saul was what you might call a high-powered executive. In fact, he was a king in Israel, which was as high up the ladder as any CEO could go. For many years Saul had taken advice from Samuel, the head of the board of directors, but Samuel had died, leaving Saul to his own devices (or vices). At first, Saul followed Samuel's counsel and banned all the wizards and mediums and their seminars from the executive board room.

However, a rival company, Philistines, Inc., moved into town and threatened Saul's empire. When he saw how much corporate power the Philistines wielded, he almost had a heart attack. (The episode is related in chapter 28 of his bestselling biography, 1 Samuel.)

So Saul put his head down on his polished desk, turned off the intercom, and prayed. "Lord, tell me what to do. Philistines, Inc., will ruin me. Give me an answer."

But the phone didn't ring, the fax was silent. The Lord didn't send a message. Saul moaned, "If only Samuel were here . . . he'd know what to do."

Saul sent for his top vice presidents and said, "Bring me a psychic or a medium . . . someone to give me advice. Keep this strictly under your hats, or none of you will have a job tomorrow."

Saul didn't realize that he would soon be out of work himself. His staff returned and told him there was a woman in the city of Endor who was a whiz at bringing back the dead. So Saul took off his navy blue double-breasted suit, put on jeans and a slouch hat, and went to visit the fortuneteller.

She was not receptive at first. "You know that King Saul has had all of the mediums and fortunetellers executed. You're a spy!"

"No, no, I take a solemn oath that I won't betray you." With that, he pulled a wad of bills out of his pocket and laid them on the table.

"Well, I guess we could have just a little seance," she said with a knowing smile. "Who do you want me to bring up?"

"Samuel," he said.

"You tricked me! You're sent from Saul," she shrieked and began to run for the door.

"Wait, I promise you no harm . . . what do you see?" What Saul saw next left him shaking with fear.

Samuel appeared before him and said angrily, "Why did you disturb me by bringing me back?"

Saul told him the deep trouble he was in, and he complained that God had left him and wouldn't give him an answer through either prophets or dreams.

Samuel didn't give Saul a positive answer. He told him that God had left Saul because he had been disobedient. Consequently,

Philistines, Inc., would force him into bankruptcy and Saul and sons would be completely out of business.

The end of the story is that Saul's sons died and Saul himself committed suicide.

How could a medium call up Samuel? There are a variety of explanations for this unusual experience. However, we do know this: Saul, as a business executive, a leader of a nation, forsook God and was not able to hear God's voice anymore. When he couldn't get through to God, he consulted a medium. Because of that, Saul died.

In Isaiah 8:19, the prophet said, "And when they say to you 'Seek those who are mediums and wizards, who whisper and mutter,' should not a people seek their God?"

The Number One Success Seminar

The best principles for business success are in the Word of God. The world's assessment of excelling is very different from God's. As a pastor, I have talked to men in my church who have said, "I have had a chance for advancement, but it would cost me in time away from my family and from serving God as I want to. I've turned down the promotion." That's the man who understands the real meaning of success.

When you stand before God someday, He is not going to ask how many hours you spent at the office or what success principles you learned at the latest seminar.

Men and women . . . true success is to be at peace with God and enjoying the peace of God . . . to be able to look in the mirror in the morning, regardless of where you are in business or on the corporate ladder, and know you are serving God with all your heart and honoring him with your life and abilities. That is when you are peace with yourself.

In addition to business seminars, there are many books that give us success principles for living. I have some in my library and find a few that have been very helpful. However, our discrimination needs to be sharpened again as we seek inspiration or information from our local bookstore or library.

10

SPIRIT GUIDES ON THE BOOKSHELVES

BOOKSTORES ARE GREAT PLACES to people-watch. The man in the navy blue suit and red power tie buys two Louis L'Amours, one John Grisham, and, as an afterthought, tosses in a business book to display when the boss comes to dinner.

The young mother is buried in cookbooks and childcare instructions while the children are sitting at a little table in the corner, turning pages of books on dinosaurs. Grandma examines a book on pruning roses but buys the historical romance or movie star biography. The college student bypasses the latest mystery novel he really wants and buys a computer book in simple English instead.

Bookstore owners try to make it easy for both the browser and the buyer by placing large signs over the racks to indicate subject matter. However, the category of "New Age" has been assigned to the dumpster. It is now dispersed on shelves throughout the store where the businessman, the young mother, Grandma, and the college student are looking.

The meteoric rise of a new "spiritual" genre that defies classification has been astronomical, but those authors and publishers in this mix of self-help, meditation, religion, and Eastern philosophy are establishing sales records. *Publishers Weekly* said, "The New Age handle is long gone, but there's a burgeoning market for books with a new kind of awareness." This is "Publishing for 'Spiritual Seekers.'"[1]

Many people who would not venture into a New Age or metaphysical bookstore are now buying the same books in the store at the mall or one of the discount warehouses. The New Age publishers' goal for the nineties is to find ways to blend their ideas into the general culture. What better place could there be than your local bookstore or library? Most ideas that have changed the way we act and think have come through the power of the printed word.

Mein Kampf, written by one man, forced millions into slavery and death.

The Bible, written under the inspiration of God, has directed more millions to freedom and life.

The New Spirituality is providing guidebooks for additional millions who are seeking alternative solutions to their problems.

Looking for Answers in the Religious Aisle

Let's bypass these categories: parapsychology, astrology, Tibetan/Hinduism, Tibetan/Buddhism, Zen Taoism, and Shaman in the male psyche and get to the all-encompassing subject of RELIGION. The manager of one bookstore said, "People are looking for answers on how to live their lives. Books about religion are accessible. They tell stories people can read and understand." In the secular bookstores, this topic covers everything from Bibles and a few current top Christian bestsellers to the newest hot topic . . . angels.

Books about angels are appearing on the religious bestseller list in celestial multitudes. With sales nearing five million copies by the middle of 1994, they are an industry all their own. With a few exceptions, these angelic encounters snatch a victim from impending disaster or warn of danger. They allow the person declared clinically dead to watch himself die—but live again to tell the story. They describe a variety of unexplained "angel" phenomena that are gripping, intriguing, and touching, but there's a warning light blinking on this bookshelf: Approach with caution.

Do I believe in angels? Yes, but not because I have seen one.

Do I believe angels can accompany us into heaven? Yes, but not because I've been there.

Do I believe in angels because of my own or someone else's experience? No, I believe in angels because the Bible tells of their power (see Matt. 26:53 and 2 Pet. 2:11, for example) and intervention in the lives of God's people (see Acts 12:7; 27:23–24). I believe in angels because God has used them for His purposes on earth and throughout eternity (see Col. 1:16).

An angel announced the birth of John the Baptist (Luke 1:19) and told Mary she would bear a son, Jesus the Messiah, (see Luke 1:30–33). An angel rolled away the stone from the tomb of Jesus (see Matt. 28:2). Angels will accompany Him when He comes again (see Matt. 16:27). Angels are mentioned more than three hundred times in the Old and New Testaments.

I believe in angels because the Bible says, "He shall give His angels charge over you, to keep you in all your ways" (Ps. 91:11).

Crash Course in Real Angels

Scripture gives us a look into the realm of angels. God's angels have specific qualities and purposes. We should be like the people who examine money for counterfeit bills and know how to be discerning by a critical study of the genuine article.

Angels are spiritual beings, although *they can assume material substance* for a specific earthly mission assigned by God (see Heb. 1:13–14, Num. 22:22–31, and Gen. 18:2–8).

Angels are sexless, but they are capable of showing emotion (see Matt. 22:30 and Luke 15:10).

Angels are immortal (see Luke 20:36).

Angels minister to believers, providing guidance, support, protection, deliverance, and comfort (see 1 Kings 19:5–8; Ps. 34:7; Dan. 6:22; Acts 12:7–11; Acts 27:23–24).

Angels' responsibilities toward unbelievers involve destruction, cursing, and affliction (Gen. 19:1–13, Judg. 5:23, and 2 Sam. 24:15–17).

However, many of the books and the television programs some angel-books have spawned have little resemblance to the angels of the Bible. Most of the angels on the bookshelves are comforting, loving, and make no demands for personal repentance.

Who Are the Angels Watching Over Me?

The new angel craze, in many cases, is attractive to those who are intrigued by the spiritual world. It is providing temporary solace to hurting and searching people in a time of personal and world upheaval and providing spirituality without being accountable to an almighty God.

Time magazine reported a poll in its December 27, 1993, issue showing that 69 percent of Americans believe in the existence of angels, but even this secular news magazine saw some of the fallacies in recent angelology.

> In their modern incarnation, these mighty messengers and fearless soldiers have been reduced to bite-size beings, easily digested. . . . For those who choke too easily on God and his rules, theologians observe, angels are the handy compromise, all fluff and meringue, kind, nonjudgmental. And they are available to everyone, like aspirin. "Each of us has a guardian angel," declares Eileen Freeman, who publishes a bimonthly newsletter called *AngelWatch* from her home in Mountainside, New Jersey. "They're nonthreatening, wise and loving beings. They offer help whether we ask for it or not. But mostly we ignore them."

Time commented, "Only in the New Age would it be possible to invent an angel so mellow that it can be ignored."[2]

One of the top sellers on the subject of celestial encounters is *Embraced by the Light*, a book by Betty Eadie. The book had been on the *New York Times* bestseller list for more than sixty-four weeks at the time of this writing, many times rated number one. It contains a mixture of Christian language with metaphysical pantheism. In her account of her "journey beyond death," Eadie has some of the elements common to most angel books: the appearance of ministering angels, being surrounded by an ethereal light, an out-of-body experience, and a loving spirit who answers a need.

Many times these angel encounters are recalled years after their occurrence. Those who have their own angel story often say it must be true because they never could have made up the vision they saw.

Christians are flocking to bookstores to get this supposedly "Christian" book, not understanding its deceptive content. Michael Baker, a buyer in a Christian bookstore, said, "In all my years working in Christian bookstores, I've never seen such a rush of people to get a book that is supposedly 'Christian.'" He categorized *Embraced by the Light* as "spiritual poison." Baker said, "There is just enough truth mixed with love and acceptance to make it one of the most dangerous books to hit the shelves—all in the name of Jesus Christ."[3]

Eadie is a Mormon whose story began in 1973, when she allegedly died after undergoing major surgery. Seventeen years later, she wrote her book telling of her experience in transcending time and space. She relates how she felt herself growing weaker and weaker until she was no longer living. She left her body and hovered over the hospital bed until three old monks appeared who explained that they had been her guardian angels during her life on earth. Soon she found herself drawn through a dark tunnel at an incredible speed until she was "embraced by the light" of a man whose whole body had a golden halo around it. From there on, Eadie describes her experience with "Jesus" and how He revealed the secrets of heaven and the mysteries of the universe to her. In this new sphere of existence, Eadie describes some of the spiritual knowledge that was conveyed to her. For instance: "All religions upon the earth are necessary because there are people who need what they teach." She says that as an individual raises his or her level of understanding about God, he or she will seek a different philosophy or religion.[4]

Is this true? Do all roads lead to heaven? Jesus said, "I am the way, the truth, and the life. No one comes to the Father except through Me" (John 14:6). Is Jesus telling the truth or is He a pathological liar? The choice for each individual will decide his or her eternal destiny.

Eadie says it was revealed to her that "all people as spirits in the pre-mortal world took part in the creation of the earth."

Also, "we assisted God in the development of plants and animal life that would be here."[5]

Did God need our help to create heaven and earth? "In the beginning God created . . ." (Gen. 1:1). Are we to assert that we are equal with God?

Eadie claims that "sin is not our true nature . . . because of our divine, spiritual nature we are filled with the desire to do good."[6]

The Bible says, "for all have sinned and fall short of the glory of God" (Rom. 3:23).

Eadie says that "Jesus was a separate being from God."[7]

In *Embraced by the Light*, Jesus seems to be an amiable tour guide, not the Savior of the world who died on the cross and rose again on the third day.

In another bestselling collection of angel encounters, *A Book of Angels*, Sophy Burnham writes about angels who disguise themselves as a comforting presence, a prevailing energy, or a person who relays a message or provides help in times of life-threatening emergencies. In a TV special, *In Search of Angels*, Burnham said, "It may be that humans evolve into angels after we die, after many lifetimes of living and dying." Burnham combined reincarnation belief with angel encounters. A narrator on the same show said, "Angels have majesty and omniscience."[8]

Only God is omniscient. To place angels on the same level as God is angel worship.

Why is there such a similarity in these accounts of angel-encounters? A person is in immediate danger—the swimmer too far from shore, the plane lost in the fog, the child bitten by a deadly snake, the woman losing her grip on a rock and about to fall from a sheer cliff—then a rescuer appears, either in the form of a real person or a figure obscured by a bright light. By the time the victim realizes he or she is saved, the rescuer has disappeared. Different stories, but a common theme.

The New Spirituality's angel fascination is an easy, warm, undemanding faith that mixes truth and myth in a clouded concoction.

In her book *Touched by Angels*, Eileen Freeman writes passionately about angels. She professes to pray to Jesus, who she believes is God in human form, but at the same time she says, "You should make your prayer to the highest Source you acknowledge outside yourself."[9]

Freeman also says, "For both the orthodox believer and the New Age adept, the message and presence of the angels in our lives are important. Angels transcend every religion, every philosophy, every creed. In fact, angels have no religion."[10]

It is true that all religions have their "angels." However, since angels are created by the only true God of the Bible, they cannot serve an idol, a false belief, or a false god. Therefore, any "angels" that come through false belief are demons and come from *their* leader, Satan, the "angel of light" (see 2 Cor. 11:14).

Joining the plethora of encounters, experiences, and explanations in the increasing angelmania is a classic that is making a timely comeback. Billy Graham's book *Angels, God's Secret Agents,* first published in 1975, gives his biblical perspective on this important and fascinating subject. One concept in his book is clear: He does not speak of angels ministering to nonbelievers. Instead, Graham wrote, "The Scriptures are full of dramatic evidences of the protective care of angels in their earthly service *to the people of God*" (emphasis mine),[11] and "Angels will minister to all the *heirs of the faith*."[12]

According to biblical teaching, the only work that angels perform regarding unbelievers is that of: (1) announcing God's judgments to them (see Gen. 19:13 and Rev. 14:6–7), (2) inflicting God's punishment (see Acts 12:23), and (3) acting as reapers in separating the sons of the kingdom, God's children, from the sons of the wicked one, the devil, at the end of the age (see Matt. 13:39).

"In choosing to follow Jesus Christ we also choose the protective watch and care of the angels of heaven. In the time of the Second Coming, we will no longer be afforded the privilege of choice. If we delay now, it will be too late, and we forfeit forever the gracious ministry of angels and the promise of salvation to eternal life."[13]

The writer of the book of Hebrews tells of the superiority of Jesus to the angels (see Heb. 1:4) and concludes that angels are "all ministering spirits sent forth *to minister for those who will inherit salvation*" (v. 14, emphasis mine).

The New Spirituality does not recognize that a prerequisite for ministering angels is to accept the free offer of salvation by accepting Jesus Christ as Savior. This is why I said to approach the current angelology with caution.

Experienced Guides

The general fascination with experience-oriented stories has generated another wave of spiritually-inspired books. The question we need to ask is, what spirit? With the exception of books on authentic Christianity, many of these experiential books are inspired by occultic, demonic forces.

One popular bestseller is Marianne Williamson's *A Return to Love*. Williamson is described in the promotional pieces as "a powerful voice of her generation, bringing spiritual solace and hope to millions." Her rise to fame was meteoric after she officiated at the wedding ceremony for Elizabeth Taylor and Larry Fortensky and was interviewed by Oprah Winfrey on her talk show. Oprah announced that she was so moved by Williamson's book that she bought a thousand copies to give to her friends.

The wife of a Christian publisher told her husband that she had just read the most fascinating book, *A Return to Love*. She praised it as a different concept of looking at God's plan for our lives. How many others, simply because Christian terminology is used, have a veil over their eyes about Satan's deceptive tactics?

Basic to Williamson's concept of love is the tenet that "we are all part of a vast sea of love, one indivisible divine mind." She emphasizes that "the love in one of us is the love in all of us. There's actually no place where God stops and you start, and no place where you stop and I start."[14]

Isn't that the return of the old pantheism?

The inspiration for Williamson's book, as well as for Gerald Jampolsky's *Letting Go of Fear* and others in the same category, was *A Course in Miracles* (to be described further in chapter 12), written by Helen Schucman, a psychologist who served as the channel for an inner voice that dictated the *Course* to her between 1965 and 1972. The deceptiveness of this spirit-guided tome, as well as its appeal to naive Christians, is that Schucman says the voice that channeled the *Course* was Jesus. Williamson believes in Jesus, but he is certainly not the Jesus of the Bible. According to Williamson, "Enlightened beings—Jesus and others—exist in a state that is only potential in the rest of us."

Also, "Jesus and other enlightened masters are our evolutionary elder brothers."[15]

"The word Christ is a psychological term. No religion has a monopoly on the truth. Christ refers to the common thread of divine love that is the core and essence of every human mind," according to Williamson.[16]

Williamson's view of God is: "God remains who He is and always will be: He is the energy, the thought of unconditional love. He cannot think with anger or judgment."

Her concept of the Holy Spirit is: "The Holy Spirit was God's answer to the ego. He is God's eternal communication link with His separated sons, a bridge back to gentle thoughts, the Great Transformer of Perception from fear to love."[17]

However, as the Bible tells us, Jesus is not an "enlightened master." He is the only begotten Son of God the Father. He was sent to earth, where He lived and taught and died on the cross for our sins and then rose from the dead. If we believe in Him, we have eternal life. The proper understanding of Jesus Christ is a mark of genuine Christianity:

> By this you know the Spirit of God: Every spirit that confesses that Jesus Christ has come in the flesh is of God, and every spirit that does not confess that Jesus Christ has come in the flesh is not of God. And this is the spirit of the Antichrist, which you have heard was coming, and is now already in the world. (1 John 4:2–3)

God is not energy; He is the Creator of the universe, the eternal, omnipotent God of heaven and earth. His name appears 3,979 times in the Scriptures as not only the God of love, but also the God of judgment. "Surely He is God who judges in the earth" (Ps. 58:11).

The Holy Spirit is not the "Great Transformer of Perception," but the third person of the Trinity, who dwells in those who have accepted Jesus Christ as their Savior.

When Jesus was preparing His disciples for His departure, He promised that another Helper would come to them:

> And I will pray the Father, and He will give you another Helper, that He may abide with you forever—the Spirit of truth, whom the world cannot receive, because it neither sees Him nor knows Him; but you know Him, for He dwells with you and will be in you. (John 14:16–17)

Also, Jesus gave the Great Commission to the church in every age: "Go therefore and make disciples of all the nations, baptizing them in the name of the Father and of the Son and of the Holy Spirit" (Matt. 28:19).

The Bible has the clearest explanation of God, Jesus, and the Holy Spirit. *A Course in Miracles* and its followers, such as Williamson, have distorted, confused, and misrepresented these truths in an unbelievable way.

When men and women come from Christian backgrounds and nod in agreement with heresies taught by followers of the New Spirituality, they are fulfilling a biblical prophecy. "Now the Spirit expressly says that in latter times some will depart from the faith, giving heed to deceiving spirits and doctrines of demons" (1 Tim. 4:1).

One who reads these books that describe a person's search for inner peace and happiness is looking for answers to life's eternal questions: Who am I? Why am I here? Where am I going? When a person attempts to find answers from writers who use spirit-channeled books, even when the spirit purports to be Jesus, they are delving into demonic areas.

The apostle Paul said, "There are some who trouble you and want to pervert the gospel of Christ. But even if we, or *an angel from heaven*, preach any other gospel to you than what we have preached to you, let him be accursed" (Gal. 1:7–8, emphasis mine).

Boomers and Books

Trendsetters in the publishing industry see the mainstreaming of New Age books as an indication that metaphysical and spiritual books will increase in popularity as we approach the new millennium. Baby boomers, over seventy-eight million of them, have reached midlife at a time when there is no indication that our economic and social crises will lessen. In their search for spirituality, they can find it promoted along with diet, health, environmentalism, and salesmanship.

Paul Elie, writing in *Publishers Weekly*, interviewed metaphysical and spiritual editors and publishers and asked what they saw on the horizon for their book products. A cross section of their comments gives us an idea of their orientation for the future.

"I find the end of the millennium personally upsetting to many people. Lately we've been getting lots of manuscripts on how to change your life—in ways that haven't really been tried before."

Speaking about the baby boomers, one editor said, "Right around the turn of the millennium they'll be going through their midlife crises, whether they like it or not. This will prompt them to undertake some inner searching—not the least the search for spiritual guides to lead them out of the wilderness of midlife."

"We're very interested right now in books that focus on the breakdown of Judeo-Christian structures . . . books about the healing issues involved [with those who are rejecting their religious past]."[18]

Many Christians are confused about this new surge in spirituality. Is a book that "sounds Christian" to be accepted as gospel truth? Should we pass this book to a hurting friend? How can we be discerning?

The author, the publishing house, and the endorsements on the cover should be indications of the spiritual content of a book. However, even those sources may experience creeping heresy. I believe that study of the Scripture and doctrines of the Christian faith are the greatest sources of spiritual health.

Solomon said, "And further, my son, be admonished by tnese. Of making many books there is no end, and much study is wearisome to the flesh" (Eccles. 12:12).

Let the buyer beware.

11

GODDESS OF MOTHER EARTH

ONE NIGHT I HAD A DREAM that I was branded an eco-villain. Someone spied me throwing a soda can into the trash barrel! I put potato peelings down the disposal and dumped grass clippings in the garbage. If that wasn't bad enough, a tree in the backyard had grown so large that it was threatening to topple into our bedroom, so I cut it down. The worst infraction of political-correctness was my neglect to mention Earth Day in our church bulletin.

When I awakened, I realized it had been a nightmare and that recycling, composting, and using only one bag at the grocery checkout had become a habit with us. Why are many in the environmental movement making Christians the bad guys in the eco-war?

The late Francis Schaeffer, one of the keenest Christian intellectuals, said that the accusations of some environmentalists was that "Christianity taught that man had dominion over nature and so man has treated nature in a destructive way."[1]

God did give man dominion over nature. In Genesis 1:28, He said, "Fill the earth and subdue it; have dominion over the fish of the sea, over the birds of the air, and over every living thing that moves on the earth."

However, the earth and all of nature belong to God, not for us to exploit, but as things borrowed or held in trust. Man's dominion is under God's dominion. "Since the Fall man has exercised this dominion wrongly. . . . Surely then, Christians, who have returned through the work of the Lord Jesus Christ to fellowship with God, and have a proper place of reference to the God who is there, should demonstrate a proper use of nature."[2]

The Garden of Eden was perfect in every way, a paradise that can only be imagined by our finite minds. However, as soon as Adam and Eve ate that first tempting morsel, the paradise was polluted.

I believe I live in one of the most beautiful areas in the world. Within a few miles I can stroll the beaches of the Pacific or breathe the brisk air of the mountains. But I can also inhale the fumes of the freeway and decry the mutilation of buildings and cliffs by graffiti.

It has taken just a few decades to contaminate the great waterways of the world, only a century since the industrial revolution to dirty the land with the ugliness of smoke and smog. However, the intrepid searchers for killers of the earth have sometimes painted the true culprits with the same lead-tainted paintbrush as the person who is just trying to live a responsible life.

Who is guilty of ravaging the earth? Accusations have been leveled against the industrialists, the lumber industry, the hunters, the chemical manufacturers, even the mother who uses disposable diapers. For some radical environmentalists, it's the influence of Christianity on our culture that is the culprit. According to these fault-finders, the Christian belief in the "divine right of man" to rule nature leads directly to man's destruction of nature.

It is irresponsible to indict all Christians as the culprits in environmental indifference. It's like the mailman who believes all dogs are vicious because he was nipped in the leg by a dachshund. Christians, of all people, should not be destroyers of nature, but builders; we are called to be good stewards of God's creation.

The Blame Game

In some ways, all of us contribute to "earthcrimes." We create tons of waste material by just living. It's only been in the past few years, however, that even garbage has gone public. When I was a boy, the city dump existed, but no one paid much attention to it except the faithful trash collectors who clattered and banged the cans in the early dawn. Those gigantic trash truck scoops, like monstrous tongues, caused the little kids to shudder when they tossed the smelly stuff up in the air, over the top, and into the back of their trucks. As the landfills began to overflow and pollution developed into a major health problem, the public became outraged.

When the media step in to support a cause, accusations and denials fly. Ecocrimes are exposed and tried on television and in the newspapers, and the culprits are sentenced without reprieve. Tal Brooke, writing about *The Ecological Great Awakening*, said, "The stakes are by no means small. The direction that public passions take could determine how we live in the Western world. It will continue to affect laws; it will affect our quality of life. It will continue to fuel the search for a perpetrator guilty of 'killing the earth.'"[3]

We can get aroused by the real eco-villains like Saddam Hussein, who ignited over a thousand Kuwaiti oil wells to poison the skies over the Persian Gulf region, or the captain of the *Exxon Valdez* supertanker, who was reportedly drunk when his massive ship collided off the Alaska coast and spilled thousands of tons of oil. However, others have been branded with crimes that are unsubstantiated. Apple growers were in financial jeopardy when a boycott was declared on their crops because a spray containing alar was accused of causing cancer. (It was later discovered that it was far less toxic than thousands of naturally produced carcinogens.) The lumber industry was portrayed as greedy and self-serving for cutting trees and destroying the spotted owls. (Only a few years ago, lumberjacks represented the mainline, hard-working American.)

We face actual and contrived environmental crises and sometimes find it difficult to separate the two. We know there are legitimate public concerns about pollution and the environment, but once again, the agendas of both the New Spirituality and the social planners should be examined for their goals. One's goal is the worship of the earth, and the other is the aim of global unity.

The main candidates for the ecological crisis have been identified as the Christian world-view, capitalism, and mega-corporations. The advantage in having a collective villain is that the social reformers can offer broad-scale remedies. History books, television shows, documentaries, and movies can be revised to declare who has caused the problem.

Look at the way some ecologists have twisted history to fit their agenda. When I was growing up, children learned about George Washington and the cherry tree story as an object lesson in integrity and honesty. Today, politically correct educators can show us the seeds of environmental destruction in young George's Western Protestant roots. The historical revisionists can turn heroes into antiheroes.

It has also been easy to accuse capitalism of generating the bulk of the problem. Some large companies have been guilty of dumping waste in the rivers or spewing toxic fumes; therefore the accusers can recommend social change, government regulations, and global cooperation.

Save the Earth

In 1989 I received an invitation to join in launching a "Campaign for the Earth." It said that leaders from around the world were going to meet in Sedona, Arizona (mecca for New Age followers) to plan the groundwork for what they called a "New World Strategy." It claimed it was *not* an organization but a "ten-year strategy to heal and evolve ourselves and the Earth. Together, we will co-create a peaceful, sustainable world by committing to a great sense of inner peace and joining together in cooperative action."

The goal was to feed the hungry, plant trees, and recycle. The information packet included World Healing Meditation, Earth Concert, U.S. Action Guide, participation at sacred sites, and more.

I didn't accept the invitation, and I don't know if their campaign got off the ground.

Other environmental strategists have launched very successful campaigns. On Earth Day 1990 it was estimated that two hundred million participants in 140 countries were involved in environmental demonstrations. In Washington, D.C., a rally took place in which 350,000 people came to participate. Tom Cruise, John Denver, Olivia Newton-John, and Richard Gere arrived to pressure politicians to use sensible environmental standards "in the now-traditional show of Hollywood star power to underscore the political message."[4]

Earth Day has inspired banner headlines, marches, and rallies while demonstrators pick up trash, plant trees, and recycle garbage. All of this sounds so noble, but the leaders and social planners are using the environment as a rallying point for their agenda to establish a new world order.

The Spiritual Side of Environmentalism

Has the New Spirituality crept into the environmental movement? If Mother Earth could talk back, she would say, "You bet it has. Just look at me!"

Sam Keen, author of *Hymns to an Unknown God,* said, "Spirituality is in. Millions who have become disillusioned with a secular view of life but are unmoved by established religion in any of its institutional forms are setting out on a quest for something—some missing value, some absent purpose, some new meaning, some presence of the sacred."[5]

Keen has the answer for "value, purpose, and meaning" in life. He says, "In our time, authentic spirituality needs to be rooted in the ecological imperative."[6]

Environmentalists are those who work to solve environmental problems, such as air and water pollution, the exhaustion of natural resources, and uncontrolled population growth. Environmental problems today are big enough and serious enough to attract the type of activists who devote their time and talents to a cause. My critical concern is that environmentalism has become a secular substitute for many Americans who have rejected a personal God.

The personification of the earth is known as the Gaia theory. Gaia was the earth goddess of ancient Greek and Roman mythology—the earth mother. The term as it is used by enviro-worshipers today refers to an Eastern, pantheistic idea that the earth *is* the goddess. In this quote from a New Age publication, we can see how the worship of Mother Earth has been brought into our culture:

> Clearly, a need from within calls for our attention at this moment in evolutionary time. The call is to serve the well-being of the living planet Earth, Gaia. . . . The call is to enter into a holistic consciousness from which all peoples, all forms of life, all manner of universal manifestation are seen as interdependent aspects of one truth.[7]

On *The Earth Day Special,* which ABC aired in 1990, Mother Earth, portrayed by Bette Midler, was rushed to the hospital as a result of all the environmental pollution. The show was about individuals making new commitments to do their part in healing Mother Earth.

It seems such a contradiction for those who consider themselves too sophisticated to believe in the infallibility of the Bible and our Father God to wholeheartedly embrace Mother Earth.

To further the case for the New Spirituality in the environment, secular humanist Carl Sagan, at the "Global Forum of Spiritual and Parliamentary Leaders on Human Survival" in Moscow in 1990, "issued a declaration that called for a '*spiritually wise,* technologically sound, ethical and farsighted stewardship of the planet' to reverse what they term the 'Crimes against Creation'" (emphasis mine).[8]

A New Constitution

Did you know that there is a *Constitution for the Federation of the Earth?* Neither did I until the voluminous document showed up in my mail. This world constitution would supplant the U.S. Constitution and the sovereignty of every other nation. Listen to its purpose:

> Under the existing circumstances of global anarchy, of political turmoil in many parts of the world, of the suppression of non-functioning of democratic electoral procedures

in many parts of the world as well as of the unprecedented urgencies of many growing world-wide crises requiring extraordinary measure if humanity is to survive, action has been organized by the World Constitution and Parliament Association—to attempt to convene World Constituent Assemblies for the purposes of preparing a *constitution for democratic federal world government.* (emphasis mine)[9]

What is one of the main functions of this Federation of the Earth? "To protect the environment and the ecological fabric of life from all sources of damage, and to control technological innovations whose effects transcend national boundaries, for the purpose of keeping Earth a safe, healthy and happy home for humanity."

Heading this federation, according to its goals, would be the world executive. It has, without biblical knowledge, described the office of the Antichrist, who will provide leadership in the gap provided by "global anarchy"!

The world government promoters not only see global anarchy ahead but also give dire predictions about population growth. They warn, "The earth is again poised on the brink of a global extinction crisis . . . the human population, now over five million, is expected to nearly double in the next four decades."[10]

Only the Lord knows if Planet Earth will survive the twenty-first century. If we believe some futuristic think-tankers, we don't have a chance!

Fallout from the Population Bomb

In 1980, two men, one a biologist and the other an economist, made a thousand-dollar bet about the future of the world. The biologist, Paul Ehrlich of Stanford University and author of the 1968 bestseller *The Population Bomb*, said that the world is on a disaster course as a result of rising population. The economist, Paul Simon, said since people produce most of the good things on this planet, more people can be expected to produce more good things. How could they determine the winner of that preposterous bet?

The determining factor was to be the future price of certain raw materials. Since Ehrlich claimed the population explosion would make us run out of the world's resources, Simon suggested they take certain raw materials, including grain and oil, and see if the prices go down (which would indicate an abundance of anything) or if the prices go up (which would show shortages). Price up: Ehrlich wins. Price down: Simon takes the thousand dollars.

The bet was a rare event, when two scholars were so precise on their disagreement and their prophecies could be statistically checked.

The views of Ehrlich and Simon represent two extreme and opposite views. Simon's group is appropriately called "cornucopias" because they see all of this bounty spilling out the cornucopia of human creativity in our ability to face problems and solve them. The free-market economists see the importance of leaving people with the decisions to have the number of children they want and limiting the role of government.

Ehrlich's view is of the Malthusians (named after the nineteenth-century economist Thomas Malthus) who predict misery for the human race because population will outpace food production. Biologists and political liberals who favor government intervention are generally in the Malthusian camp.

Population growth on our planet has exploded in the past few generations, yet Ehrlich's dire predictions of worldwide famine have not come true. We do know that Africa, in particular, is suffering agonies of starvation and death, but this is largely caused by war, poverty, and poor distribution. This may be a shocker, but while global population is growing like dandelions in summer, farmers have grown more food than ever.

"Food production in the developing world more than doubled between 1965 and 1990," according to population scholar John Bongaarts in the *Scientific American*.[11]

The *Scientific American* report also said that global food production is neither as grim as the pessimists believe nor as rosy as the optimists claim. So what are we to believe?

In the population debate, the specter of worldwide hunger and depletion of natural resources are cited as reasons for more government control. These were the bases for Ehrlich's and Simon's bet.

What has happened to prices, which are determined by the availability of natural resources? In the ten-year period after the original wager, the price of all five raw materials went down, even in real dollars. Ehrlich lost the bet and wrote a check to Simon for one thousand dollars.

If resource depletion is only part of the population bomb destruction, then the next step would be to equate the population explosion with poverty. However, that theory could be pretty well exploded when we see countries with comparable features—Taiwan and China, North and South Korea, and, until recently, East and West Germany. In all three sets, the country with the denser population became richer. Compare Japan at 850 people per square mile with Uganda's 200 people per square mile. One wealthy, one desperately poor. Even birth control for the Third World is not the entire answer. It must include women's education, healthcare, and economic development, which have long been the concerns and activities of Christian missionaries.

The population bomb is now aimed toward ecology. We hear about deforestation, species extinction, global warming, soil depletion, pollution. I know there are serious ecological problems around the world, but I do not believe that population control will eliminate world poverty or protect our environment.

Defusing the Population Bomb

Let's look at some of the facts about this earth's bursting at the seams. Fertility in the United States has been steadily declining for two centuries.[12] The Netherlands saw its fertility rate plunge 53 percent in just twenty years, and the French rate dropped 32 percent in eleven years.[13] In fact, even in the Third World regions of Asia, Africa, and Latin America, fertility rates are declining rapidly.

In spite of the fact that birth rates have been decreasing, many pro-abortion advocates, such as Planned Parenthood, attempt to justify their practices by appealing to the threat of a population explosion.[14] This is not, of course, the only issue used by pro-abortionists to support the mass killing of babies.

The abortion industry is nasty business. It is also a multi-million-dollar business that is a national shame. Abortion rights have divided our nation in a civil war of social, economic, political, and ethical concerns. In the forefront is the wealthy, powerful, and influential organization Planned Parenthood. In his comprehensive exposé of Planned Parenthood, George Grant wrote, "But despite this nearly omnipresent intrusion into family, church, state, and culture, Planned Parenthood has somehow managed to manufacture for itself a sterling reputation. It has brokered its abortion trade into a public image that is very nearly unassailable."[15]

Many professing Christians are in executive positions at Planned Parenthood, and many others endorse its aims. The Bible declares the sanctity of life for all: the weak and the strong, the great and the small, the rich and the poor, the lame and the whole, the young and the old, the unborn and the born. Christians who endorse and support pro-abortion (which is a simile for pro-choice) should examine their beliefs. The Bible says:

> For You formed my inward parts;
> You covered me in my mother's womb.
> I will praise You, for I am fearfully and
>   wonderfully made;
> Marvelous are Your works,
> And that my soul knows very well.
> My frame was not hidden from You,
> When I was made in secret,
> And skillfully wrought in the lowest parts of the
>   earth.
> Your eyes saw my substance, being yet
>   unformed.
> And in Your book they all were written,
> The days fashioned for me,
> When as yet there were none of them.
>   (Ps. 139:13–16)

The fallout from the population bomb and the tentacles of the New Spirituality strike not only ecology but also abortion justification. The next target is government intervention.

"The Worst Pollution," According to Gore

In a surrealist novel called *A Creed for the Third Millennium*, Colleen McCullough describes a future society where the government regulates population by enforcing one-child families. If a couple wants another child, they have to place their name in a lottery with the Second Child Bureau. The odds in that lottery are ten thousand to one.

It is a chilling thought that a birth-control program could be determined by the state, and yet that is exactly what happened in India in 1975. Indira Gandhi (no relation to Mahatma) launched an emergency measure and rounded up thousands of men for involuntary sterilization, often under unsanitary conditions. The repercussions were so strong that Gandhi was driven from office and "family planning" was given a bad name.

China has launched a brutal, one-child-per-couple policy. Planned Parenthood maintains that the communist government's genocidal approach to population control is a "model of efficiency."[16]

Although we do not have forced family planning in America, could government-sanctioned abortions be a harbinger of such an obscenity?

In his book *Earth in the Balance*, Al Gore has a chapter on material waste in which he says, "If we have come to see the things we use as disposable, have we similarly transformed the way we think about our fellow human beings?"

He laments our devaluation of "latchkey children, abandoned spouses, neglected friends and neighbors . . . especially children who are thrown out of their homes because they are too difficult to handle or because their parents no longer have the extra time for their special needs." The conclusion he reaches is that *"the worst of all forms of pollution is wasted lives."*[17]

Gore is right in his compassion for wasted lives, but how does he reconcile this concern with the wholesale legal slaughter of one and a half million unborn human beings every year in the United States? Gore needs to explain how he can speak out against ecological destruction on one hand and at the same time deny the right to live for helpless humans who have no chance to cry out to a loving God for justice.

Christian author and researcher Doug Groothuis said:

Gore is more concerned about preserving an ecological niche for the spotted owl than he is about the precarious prenatal niche of the unborn in America and throughout the planet. It is exceedingly odd that one who so adamantly argues for a greater sense of "connectedness to nature" would champion a public policy that allows the unrestricted severing of the connection between mother and child through abortion. This brutal fact alone disqualifies the Vice President from being an ecologist whose thinking is consistent with the deepest insights of Christian ethics. Prenatal ecology is not his concern.[18]

The Church Out of Focus

Many Christians have been led to think that their belief is responsible for all the eco-crises today. Mary Tucker, religion history professor at Bucknell University, said, "We have no environmental ethics that come out of a religious worldview. We could destroy the planet without a protest from the religious community." She emphasized that "A major way to change our environmental crisis is to change religious attitudes."[19]

Who started the spark of accusations and fueled the fire against Christian beliefs on the environment? Lynn White Jr., a student of medieval history, presented a paper at a meeting of the American Association for the Advancement of Science in December 1966 that was the "eco-shot heard 'round the world." White's paper became compulsory reading for anyone interested in eco-philosophy, and environmental scientists are generally introduced to White's viewpoint as part of their education. Here's a sample:

Christianity bears a huge burden of guilt. More science and more technology are not going to get us out of the present ecologic crisis until we find a new religion. . . . We shall continue to have a worsening ecologic crisis until we reject the Christian axiom that nature has no reason for existence save to serve man.[20]

With all the media coverage of Earth Day events, numerous religious leaders would have us believe we must join forces with others in this crusade to save the planet. Os Guiness, Christian intellectual and writer, once observed that the fads of the church follow the fads of the secular culture—twenty years later. Today, however, that time lag has been shortened. The organized church is racing to keep up with the latest trends, especially environmentalism.

Have Christian leaders embraced Mother Earth? One Baptist leader said, "Christians need to embrace a broader sense of salvation . . . salvation of humankind and redemption of creation." A pastor called on all members of his denomination to take the lead in a new theology of "Earth-care" because he believes we have focused on personal salvation to the neglect of society and the environment. Another pastor became president of Ted Turner's one-world group, the Better World Society. I have deliberately omitted their names for I do not wish to embarrass them if they have recanted their views now.

Something is wrong. I believe that Christians should be guardians of the environment, but if we make the environment the centerpiece of Christian attention and action, we shift the very basis of the Christian faith.

Many people have moved toward pantheism without recognizing its basic philosophy in many environmental movements. However, I believe that the environmentalists recognize it, for it is exactly what they want. Here is what Jonathan Porritt of Friends of the Earth said:

> The present threat to mankind's survival can be removed only by a revolutionary change in individual human beings. This change of heart must be inspired by religion in order to generate the willpower needed for putting arduous new ideas into practice.[21]

True change of heart can only come about through confessing our sins and accepting Jesus Christ as Savior. The Bible says, "For with the heart one believes unto righteousness, and with the mouth confession is made unto salvation" (Rom. 10:10).

Writing in *Psychology Today*, Dr. Eugene Taylor said "Today's spiritual awakening not only reveals the hidden interconnectedness of things, it prompts people to pledge themselves to a host of new causes, from saving the planet to helping the disenfranchised. . . . As Gandhi proclaimed, we might live to see even governmental service become the new form of spiritual discipline."[22]

Christians, we should be wary of joining forces with any group or movement that promotes the worship of Earth, rather than the worship of the Creator. By making the environment the center of Christian attention and action, we fall into the same category of those whom Paul was castigating in Romans 1:25 when he stated there were those who "exchanged the truth of God for a lie, and worshiped and served the creature rather than the Creator."

Guardians of God's Earth

God's creation is awesome. To catch a glimpse of a hummingbird or watch an eagle swoop to its nest illustrates the Lord's attention to small and large details. The ant and the elephant. The ostrich and the giraffe. The dachshund and the Great Dane. How amazing is the mind of God!

Standing at the rim of the Grand Canyon, we hear many voices say, reverently or irreverently, "Oh my God!" The cobalt blue of the Caribbean, the emerald green of Hawaii, the stark white of Alaska, or the gold of an autumn tree in Vermont, God painted our earth in every shade imaginable.

When I was in the hospital at the Mayo Clinic in October of 1994, my world was painted with the colors of pale green and white; the monotony was broken only when my beautiful wife and family came to see me. I had arrived as a strong, seemingly healthy person and left with an unexpected prognosis and the anticipation of six months of chemotherapy. I shall never forget the words of my doctor: "David, you will never look at the ocean in the same way again."

It only takes a prison, a hospital, or a natural disaster to make us view our family, friends, and the world around from a new perspective.

David the psalmist wrote:

> When I consider Your heavens,
>   the work of Your fingers,
> The moon and the stars, which
>   You have ordained,
> What is man that You are mindful of him,
> And the son of man that You visit him? . . .
> You have made him to have
>   dominion over the works of
>   Your hands;
> You have put all things under his feet,
> All sheep and oxen—
> Even the beasts of the field,
> The birds of the air,
> And the fish of the sea
> That pass through the paths of seas.
>
> O Lord, our Lord,
> How excellent is Your name in all the earth!
>   (Ps. 8:3–4, 6–9)

When Christians love God, they love what He has made. *Yes, Doctor, I'll never look at the ocean in the same way again.*

What We Can Do

We show our love for the environment and its creatures in many ways. One example is that of Dr. Ann Croissant, professor of education at Azusa Pacific University. With a family and a full-time university position, Dr. Croissant saw the encroachment of urban sprawl as an opportunity to show Christian stewardship—God's charge to us that we be responsible caretakers of each other and the earth. "Moreover it is required in stewards that one be found faithful" (1 Cor. 4:2).

With a dream and the goal "to breathe life into what I teach—to impart the value of service-learning, leadership and stewardship," Dr. Croissant spearheaded the Glendora (California) Community Conservancy. The conservancy purchases important wildlife and open-space land, protects endangered species, and establishes conservation and recreation areas. Croissant said, "We expect networks of wildlife corridors, trails, bikeways, and high-tech education centers in the future, and have plans to develop stewardship curricula for schools and organizations."[23]

Ann's idea, with Christian commitment and no government help, is just an example of what environmental stewardship is all about.

Christians who love God and all He has made should, of all people, treat nature with an overwhelming respect. We must show our care in practical ways, not only because it is our God-given responsibility, but also because it is a witness to our humanistic friends that we put love into action.

Francis Schaeffer said, "We have to be in the right relationship with Him in the way He has provided, and then, as Christians, have and practice the Christian view of nature"[24]

God uses creative people to solve environmental problems to find cures for plagues, to grow better crops. We can choose environmentally safe household products and grow our own vegetables without the need to pledge allegiance to Mother Earth. We can love and protect animals but still eat meat. We have our personal God-given rights to determine family planning, and we do not need government intervention. We can be anti-pollution without putting "Save the Earth" bumper stickers on our cars.

Although we have an environmental crisis, the world has a worse sin crisis. We are experiencing today the acceleration of evil: the wars and rumors of wars, famines, pestilences, and earthquakes that Jesus said were the signs of the times and the end of the age (see Matthew 24).

The believers in Jesus Christ will someday see the world as it was in the beginning. . . Paradise regained. Jesus said, "Behold, I make all things new" (Rev. 21:5).

The good news is:

> The day of the Lord will come as a thief in the night,
> in which the heavens will pass away with a great noise, and
> the elements will melt with fervent heat; both the earth

and the works that are in it will be burned up. Therefore, since all these things will be dissolved, what manner of persons ought you to be in holy conduct and godliness, looking for and hastening the coming of the day of God, because of which the heavens will be dissolved, being on fire, and the elements will melt with fervent heat? Nevertheless we, according to His promise, look for new heavens and a new earth in which righteousness dwells. (2 Pet. 3:10–13)

What a great Earth Day that will be!

12

INSIDE THE
CHURCH DOOR

I USED TO GO TO CHURCH, BUT I always went home on Sunday feeling so guilty that it was like lead in my stomach the rest of the week. It just seemed to me that a God who would make me feel that way was not the God I was looking for."

Rex was an attractive, well-dressed man in his early forties with a movie-star smile. He was greeting the people who were arriving en masse to what used to be a theater, now converted to a comfortable, tastefully decorated meeting hall. In the foyer was a box that said, "Seven-dollar donation suggested." Beside the box, neatly arranged brochures announced "A Course in Miracles."

My co-author, Carole, went to the meeting with a notepad and some apprehension. Knowing the occult foundations of the Course in Miracles, she wondered what she would encounter.

Carole lingered at the door to talk with Rex as the attendees streamed in. "Do most of the people who attend the Course belong to a church?" Carole asked.

"Almost all of them did at one time, but they became sick of the guilt trip or the lack of caring. This is our 'church' now, if you want to call it that. Is this your first time here?" Rex was like a charming host at a newcomers tea.

"Yes it is. I heard about the course and was interested in finding out more." Carole knew she was being greeted as a potential recruit.

"You're going to love it. I've been coming for over three years. James is a marvelous teacher—he used to be a woman, you know."

"Very interesting." Carole walked quickly to take a seat before her expression could betray her feelings.

It was a weeknight, but the auditorium and balcony were filled in about ten minutes until there were more than three hundred people, with standing room only. With the well-dressed, polite crowd, it could have been a Baptist Church in a secular setting. But the service was far from orthodox.

When a beautiful blonde-haired woman, the course coordinator, took the microphone behind a transparent podium, a hush fell over the crowd as she instructed the audience to deep-breathe. Her voice was soothing; soft mood music was played by a young man with a flute. Eyes closed, arms at their sides, the participants meditated while Ms. Blonde led them mentally through quiet meadows and infinite skies. As Carole looked around the room, she was grateful that she didn't meet any other inquisitive eyes. Her son-in-law, Rick, who had accompanied her to the meeting, had his eyes wide open, staring straight ahead.

James, who spoke for an hour and a half without notes and never lost the crowd's attention, was a handsome man wearing a black turtleneck shirt and jeans. He moved like a dancer and used the cynical humor of a professional satirist. His communication skills were honed to perfection. Every gesture, every intonation, seemed carefully studied.

"The Course in Miracles is about the experience of love. We are here to tell you how to be free of guilt and practice forgiveness. Every religion has a story of original guilt. I was raised in the Catholic Church by Catholic nuns. Talk about guilt!"

The audience laughed like they were cued for a television sitcom.

"That Adam and Eve ate of the tree of guilt is insane. The God of the Old Testament is completely insane. Guilt is bred into us, but the Course in Miracles is a radically new thought system that says everything we have been taught was wrong." More laughter. James was just getting started.

"God didn't make the world, and God didn't make your body; but He can use your body. We are a part of the world we made, and we can change that world." *Applause.*

"In the new priesthood, we are all ministers. Coffee shops are the new confessionals . . . we're all forgiving each other."

As Carole scribbled notes, the girl next to her shifted slightly to avoid the intrusion of this activity.

"The purpose of the Course in Miracles," James emphasized, "is to know that it is God's will to make you happy."

James gave a parting admonition before the final meditation and prayer: "Repeat over and over again, 'I'm an innocent child of God. I'm an innocent child of God.'"

No one else moved during meditation, but Carole and Rick made a hasty retreat while everyone's eyes were closed. Ms. Blonde, who was standing in back of the room, glanced up to give them a disapproving look.

It's been more than twenty years since the book *A Course in Miracles* was channeled into the world through Helen Schucman, who claimed it was Jesus who gave her these principles. Why is it having such an upsurge now?

As secularism invades our churches, the sovereign God of the Bible has been dethroned and replaced by self-directed religion, do-it-yourself rituals, and morality based on feelings. The people attending A Course in Miracles are like many who are spiritually hungry and seeking to find the power that only Jesus can fill when He said, "I have come that they may have life, and that they may have it more abundantly" (John 10:10).

The Boomers Are Shopping

As the baby boomers reach middle age, they are prominent members of a spiritually starved generation. Many have teenagers who are questioning their grandparents' beliefs or their parents' lack of belief. *How do we answer the kids if we don't have any answers of our own?*

Prayer is one answer, and if we believe the polls, more Americans are praying today. "According to recent studies by Andrew Greeley, the sociologist-novelist-priest, more than 78 percent of all Americans pray at least once a week; more than 57 percent report praying at least once a day. Greeley finds that even among the 13 percent of Americans who are atheists or agnostics, nearly one in five still pray daily."[1]

Books on prayer are major league today. "After the Bible," says Werner Mark Link, president of Crossroad, a publisher of religious books, "books on prayer are our biggest sellers."[2]

Our question should be, "Who are people praying to?" Jesus tells us to pray to "our Father who art in heaven." But prayers are also offered to Allah, Buddha, the "Higher Power," the "Universal Force," and the "Man Upstairs."

Jesus said to ask "in *My* name" (John 14:14).

All through this book we have been saying that spirituality is "in." Church historian Martin Marty notes that in the 1960s the word *spiritual* had lost meaning and relevance for modern culture. Marty says, "The 'old piety,' was passé. Now spirituality is back, almost with a vengeance. . . . I find myself treating the concern for spirituality as an event of our era."[3]

The New Spirituality as a religion is like a gigantic Tinkertoy going in all directions, ready to topple and collapse when the next piece is added. It is a collection of thoughts, therapies, and techniques that are presented cafeteria-style to starved seekers. Believers and nonbelievers alike are being sold spiritual junk food. People may taste of guided visualization, art therapy, aromatherapy, therapeutic touch, inward harmony, metaphysics, or inner healing. These things may seem to satisfy for a time, but they will not contribute to healthy growth.

We'll describe just two examples of the New Spirituality in both the pulpit and the pews. More are making inroads, if people are discerning enough to see.

Hazards of Inner Healing

A woman was invited by a pastor to speak at his church and tell her remarkable story of healing. She told of a long bout with physical and mental illnesses. She spoke with such convincing pathos that many in the spellbound congregation of this main-line, evangelical church were convinced that if they weren't healed it was their own spiritual problem. The fault was usually attributed to a lack of forgiveness toward someone who had caused a traumatic or negative experience in their lives.

In the congregation was one woman who had had a severe physical problem for twenty years. She believed God could heal her if He chose but instead had strengthened her through her pain and given her a special ministry to others who were disabled. She was deeply hurt to be told that the reason she wasn't healed was because of her lack of faith.

The woman speaker who practiced inner healing used her own personal experience as doctrinal truth. The controversy caused by this teaching was destructive and divisive in that body of believers.

Whenever we receive teaching in spiritual matters, we should know the origins and theological beliefs of the teachers. Sometimes we are more careful of examining the ingredients in what we eat than we are in what we are told by spiritual "experts."

We do not wish to indict anyone's character or imply that anyone lacks concern for others. Some of these proponents of inner healing may be loving, convincing, or just plain misguided. However, if a charge against a killer is murder, manslaughter, or carelessness, the result is still the death of a human being. In the realm of the spirit, the consequences of false teaching are the same: spiritual death.

Inner healing is sometimes called "healing of the memories," "healing of the emotions," "spiritual healing," or "soul healing." It is a "psychological technique whereby a person seeks to overcome negative human emotions while reaffirming positive attitudes towards self and others. The negative emotions with which inner healing deals are primarily guilt, anger, fear, self-hatred or hatred of others, envy, lack of self-confidence or self-esteem."[4]

Agnes Sanford is considered the forerunner of what is known today as "inner healing" and/or "healing of the memories." Sanford, a student of psychology who was heavily influenced by

Carl Jung, was a charismatic Episcopalian and wife of a missionary. After being healed of an acute depression, she became involved in healing the mental and physical ills of others.[5]

Sanford was a pantheist who wrote, "God is actually *in* the flowers and the growing grass and all the little chirping, singing things. He made everything out of Himself and then He put a part of Himself into everything."[6]

If Sanford had such a faulty concept of God, she also was biblically wrong about her methodology of teaching. She wrote, "The healing Spirit of God is in the wind and the sun and the little creeping things upon the earth, and is most certainly available to the one who prays with faith, be he minister or layman, man, woman, or child."[7]

In her writings, Sanford also mentioned a "messenger of light" who might lift us out of darkness into immortality. The only person the Bible describes as a messenger (or angel) of light is Satan!

Since her theology was corrupt, the churches of today should avoid the teachings of her followers.

Although Sanford is most responsible for introducing inner healing to the church, it was the late Ruth Carter Stapleton, sister of former President Jimmy Carter, who was influential in spreading the practice through mainline denominations and charismatic churches. During the presidency of Jimmy Carter, the term "born again" became a frequently used and even secularized term. Riding the wave of popularization was Stapleton, who used the term to give plausibility to her inner healing work within the Christian community. She was asked to speak at churches and had books released by Christian publishers, which gave further credibility to her practices.

Stapleton, with her compassion to help people overcome emotional problems, had a strange interpretation of what it means to be "born again." She would say that all religions have their meaning for being born again. A person could look at a beautiful picture or hear some inspiring music and be born again. The question of sin and repentance was not an issue, except as a barrier to the belief in one's inherent goodness.

One technique that Mrs. Stapleton used in her teaching meditation exercises was "faith imagination." She had her subjects regress in their imaginations to their childhood, even to the stage when they were merely fetuses in their mothers' wombs. Urging them to imagine those instances when they incurred the hurts they were trying to overcome, she told them to imagine Jesus loving the person who had hurt them and then, in their minds, to reach out to those persons with forgiveness.

She claimed that anyone, Christians, non-Christians, or atheists, could receive inner healing by using faith imagination.

"Mrs. Stapleton claimed to use faith imagination to bring people in therapy into an experience of the 'divine creative power of perfect love.' To her, the 'healing creative energy' that sets us free is embodied in Jesus Christ. She said, 'It's possible to see this divine love in whatever way, shape, or form we want to.'"[8] Ruth Carter Stapleton's view of man's alleged divine potential, her concept of what it means to be "born again," and her affinity for psychological practices mixed with Christian metaphors are not biblical standards.

You may be saying, "Wait a minute, Dr. Jeremiah. What does that have to do with us today?"

Inner healing is in our churches today, a New Spirituality that replaces God's healing powers with man's ability to heal himself through psychological guidance. There is no doubt that people are often healed of many sicknesses, emotional and physical, through mind science and even witchcraft. But these have nothing to do with the spiritual healing that only God through Jesus Christ can accomplish.

The Bible says, "Bless the LORD, O my soul, and forget not all His benefits: Who forgives all your iniquities, Who heals all your diseases" (Ps. 103:2–3).

Spiritual Growth or Spiritual Confusion?

Another church-sponsored practice called Momentus was started by Dan Tocchini, a professed born-again believer. He had worked for Lifespring, a New Age organization similar to est, and brought many of Lifespring's techniques into a church setting in order to promote Christian spiritual growth. Such techniques were described this way by one observer:

"For four days, they blurt out secrets, slug pillows while yelling 'Mama, Mama,' and pretend to be aboard a sinking cruise ship that has only one life raft.

"They also listen to music from the television show *Beverly Hills, 90210* and—occasionally—claim to hear whisperings from God. By the time it's over, many say that they've never felt closer to Jesus or to other people, and that their lives have dramatically changed."[9]

Controversy over Momentus arises from methods used, such as the "living mirror" exercise, in which individuals stand in front of another person and are told what those people think of them. One man told of his "mirror" encounter with another man who looked him in the face and said, "You make me want to vomit."

"'People who don't know you from Adam are giving you a rundown on what they think you are, and some of it is just really uncalled for,' says Wayne Coombs, a Palos Verdes minister who otherwise loves Momentus. 'It's said with a real sense of unkindness, and for me, there was some damage.'"[10]

Momentus training is similar to Lifespring in many ways.

Participants are sworn to secrecy. Though couched in a Christian context and endorsed by the pastors and elders of some churches, those who are involved in the seminars are not encouraged to bring or use their Bibles. Graduates recruiting others to receive the training give glowing reports of what it has done for them. One church (the home church) has split over the legitimacy of the training. The cost for the four-day training is very high (eight hundred dollars per couple in the beginning of 1994).

One Momentus graduate, we'll call her Susan, said she was very cautious and leery about enrolling, but a close friend had taken the course and it had made a profound and positive change in her life. The friend persuaded Susan to go to a "discovery meeting," where she would find out more. Susan, her husband, and teenage son signed up for the Thursday-through-Sunday session. "It was very grueling, beginning at nine in the morning and lasting until ten or eleven at night, after which you had to do homework," Susan said.

Although there was Scripture displayed around the room, there was never any praying, and people were discouraged from mentioning any Bible verses. In fact, Susan said, "We were told that Christ was a crutch.

"We were divided into groups by asking some key people to look around the room and choose the person we were least attracted to as our partner. It was embarrassing for me, and for the person I chose. I thought I would be with my husband for the sessions, but instead the woman I humiliated was my buddy for four days."

We asked Susan why she stayed, and she said, "I developed a great deal of compassion for people as they told their stories, and I thought this could be a tool to evangelize. However, I began to see how the tactics used to offend us and break us psychologically were not ways I could serve Jesus Christ."

Former members of the church where Tocchini belonged said that people who had known each other for years, who had been brothers and sisters in the Lord, were no longer speaking to one another after participating in these confrontations. In the eight-hundred-member congregation, about eighty families left when the pastor refused to condemn the Momentus seminar.

Secrecy, questionable methods, divisive tactics . . . are these the work of the Lord? What is happening to our churches when ideas come in that cause biblical doctrine to be replaced by psychological encounters and human potential methods?

"'In all my life, I've never seen people as energized as the ones from those early seminars,' says a Bible teacher and author who initially endorsed Momentus then switched sides and led the revolt at Tocchini's church. 'But it took over the energy of the church. It sucked everything into its orbit.'"[11]

Inner healing and Momentus are only two of the unorthodox movements that are slipping "inside the church door" to guide people through avenues of feelings, rather than biblical truths.

The Bible says "we should no longer be children, tossed to and fro and carried about with every wind of doctrine, by the trickery of men, in the cunning craftiness of deceitful plotting, but, speaking the truth in love, may grow up in all things into Him who is the head—Christ" (Eph. 4:14–15).

Politically Correct and Tolerant

When did the concept of being "politically correct" apply to the church? Our society has become so paranoid about genderism, ageism, and sexism that this paranoia even affects the wording in our traditional hymns. Here's one for the people in the pews:

> The Rev. James Crawford, a pastor in Boston, says his committee, which is charged with producing a new hymnal for the United Church of Christ, is seeking "what is politically correct, and what that means is to discover metaphors for Ultimate Reality that do not assume a cosmos or creation where . . . some male-like figure or being is in charge."[12]

The tongue-in-cheek comment on this news item was, "How nice it is not to have to answer to anyone except yourself! We expect that 'The Old Rugged Cross,' if not already banned by modern denominations, will be expurgated because of ageism, lookism, and religionism, and that Handel's *Messiah* will be emasculated and eviscerated thusly: 'And UR [Ultimate Reality] shall reign forever, how clever: U-top-i-a, U-top-i-a.'"

Here's another trend that seems to be gaining momentum: Have you noticed how neopaganism in the form of Native American spirituality is appearing today in movies, television, and books? I like Indian lore as much as anyone, but not enough to sanction its beliefs and rituals. Mainstream Protestant churches are endorsing forms of New Spirituality when they align themselves with the World Council of Churches that opened its last general session with a Native American cleansing ritual. At the World Congress on Religion in Chicago in 1993, major Protestant representatives signed declarations of unity with neopagan spirituality.

Do the people in the pews know what their denominational representatives are promoting?

We are told to be tolerant, not dogmatic. "After all, everyone is entitled to his own opinion." If we, as Christians, try to convey our beliefs or cite biblical principles, we may be viewed as narrow-minded and repressive. *"Don't try to shove your ideas down our throats!"*

To many, truth is very personal and entirely subjective. The Christian who gives his or her testimony may be deflected by the reply, "That's okay for you, but it's not the truth for everyone."

"Tolerance" in the church today has resulted in God's being depicted as He/She and the Virgin Mary's being described only as a "young woman."

The Jesus Seminar is a California-based group of about two hundred biblical "scholars" who attack some of Christianity's most sacred traditions.

According to the Jesus Seminar scholars:

"Jesus never claimed to be the Messiah and did not predict the end of the world.

"The Lord's Prayer, which the Bible says Jesus composed, was compiled by Christians after His death.

"A professor of biblical studies at DePaul University in Chicago said, 'The image that comes out of our work is not a Jesus who was an apocalyptic visionary as much as he was a social revolutionary.'"[13]

In a later meeting, the Jesus Seminar determined that Jesus Christ was not born of a virgin. "Twenty-five of the 26 members of the Jesus Seminar rendered that verdict late Friday after nearly five hours of debate. It came in the wake of a presentation by a feminist theologian who said the notion of a virgin birth represented another example of subjugation of women, and that Christ was, in fact, an illegitimate child."[14]

To be politically correct, we are told we must be tolerant. A religion professor at a Christian college commented on a conference on religious pluralism in which three historians talked about religion in the academy. "One, an observant Jew, another, a practitioner of Eastern spiritualism, and me, an Episcopalian . . . committed to certain academic standards and respectful interchange, discussed religion. Tolerance guided us.'

The woman professor said, "I confess that I wasn't too sure how to demonstrate my faith. I actually felt embarrassed for eating all the food and not bringing my prayer book!"[15]

Using the command in the Bible, "Judge not, lest ye be judged," the professor illustrated the oft-misused text to justify the validity of other beliefs.

What should we judge or not judge? Christians have the obligation to judge the truth or falsity in other beliefs. Likewise, we have the right to stand in judgment whenever someone claims that something is Christian. The Bible says, "holding fast the faithful word as he has been taught, that he may be able, by sound doctrine, both to exhort and convict those who contradict" (Titus 1:9).

True, we should not judge whether or not a person is a true believer. Only God knows the human heart. However, to say that we cannot judge Eastern spiritualism or any other religion is a contradiction. That judgment is not upon a person but upon the truth or error in the belief system he expounds.

The New Spirituality and the Old Truths

When we don't know the names of the people in our neighborhood, when we work in one city and live in another, when we are fed up with meetings and committees no matter how worthy the cause, we hunger for communion with God. *Does He care? Am I important to Him? Will He really hear me when I pray? Oh, God, is there anything solid in this sinking world? Where are You?*

We go to our leaders for help, and they tell us to come to church more often or take a class. The longing is still there, but it cannot be filled by a program, a tour of the Holy Land, or a course in family dynamics (or A Course in Miracles!).

To put spirituality in focus, I suggest four things:

First: *Discover what Scripture says about spirituality and explore these riches daily.* Billy Graham's daughter Anne, a gifted Bible teacher, said she put aside her Bible commentaries and books on biblical subjects, took out her Bible and notebook, and immersed herself in the Word. As she did so, she found herself returning to her first love, Jesus Christ.

Eugene Peterson, professor of spiritual theology at Regent College, said, "Spirituality that is not continuously and prayerfully soaked in the biblical revelation soon withers and hardens into self-righteousness or fragments into psychology."[16]

Second: *Avoid any manner of spirituality that does not require commitment to the true God.* Fads will come and go in the church, but a lifelong faith commitment to God as revealed in Jesus Christ is essential to true spirituality. Commitment is a commodity that is in short supply today, but the man or woman who is truly in love with Jesus will be bound to Him forever. Jesus has told us, "I will never leave you nor forsake you" (Heb. 13:5).

Although there is validity, I believe, in leaving a church where the leadership consistently presents false doctrine, I also see people who are offended by one remark from the pulpit or one perceived hurt flit to the next church to look for fault there. It's like the cartoon I saw of a skeleton dressed in women's clothes and sitting on a park bench; the caption read, "Waiting for the perfect man." There is no perfect church, either.

Third: *Seek fellowship with other Christians wherever they may be.* Sometimes we develop a denominational or congregational exclusivity that deprives the body of Christ of a strong witness. I am a Baptist, but the church I pastor does not carry the word *Baptist* in its name. While we function in every way as a Baptist congregation, we decided several years ago that it was more important to emphasize the things that united us with other believers than those few things that might separate us.

My brothers and sisters in Christ come from other backgrounds and races. While we may not agree on every minor point of doctrine or methodology, we are together in absolute loyalty to Jesus Christ and His Word. All believers are one in Christ, and inter-family squabblers are poor witnesses to the watching and skeptical world.

Fourth: *Look for mature leaders* who will guide and nurture you in the Lord. None of us is infallible, but a man or woman's spiritual maturity will be reflected in his or her personal integrity. One of the saddest things to see in our Christian churches today is the pastor or leader who is involved in open sin and, as a result, leaves a hurting flock in his trail.

Wait! . . . There's Reason to Rejoice!

After reading this manuscript before it went to the publisher, one of my friends said, "This New Spirituality thing is everywhere, isn't it?" That's the bad news. The good news is that the same spiritual hunger that is sweeping our world is also the Christian's opportunity for personal growth and outreach.

An amazing prayer movement for revival is spreading throughout America and other parts of the world like sparks in a tinder-dry forest. You probably won't read about it in your papers or see it on the television news, but Christian leaders are reporting that we may be on the brink of a great spiritual awakening, unlike anything the world has seen.

The National Day of Prayer, headed first by Vonette Bright, whose husband founded Campus Crusade for Christ, and now by Shirley Dobson, wife of Dr. James Dobson, has grown by 250 percent every year since 1991. Kay Parker, public relations head of this volunteer organization, said that if the average company grew that fast it probably couldn't keep up with demand for its products.

Promise Keepers, a special outreach to men that began in 1990 with two men, University of Colorado head football coach Bill McCartney and his friend Dr. Dave Wardell, soon had seventy-two men who gathered to pray and fast. By 1994 it had grown to 278,000 men who filled seven stadiums. In 1995, the goal of this organization is to host gatherings at twelve to fourteen sites that will draw a total of 600,000 men!

Brigadier General Dick Abel, retired, a Vietnam veteran, former special assistant to the Joint Chiefs of Staff, and now with Campus Crusade for Christ, said, "Hundreds of men and women in the military are attending Bible studies and prayer meetings. Soldiers are mentioned throughout God's Word. The Christian life, like that of a soldier's, is one of discipline. Remember that Cornelius, a soldier, was the first Gentile to became a Christian."[17]

Concerts of Prayer International was founded in 1987, dedicated to serving the church by mobilizing movements of united prayer for spiritual awakening. Its director, Steve Bell, said, "Today a global prayer movement is growing and changing so dramatically, it's more like a raging torrent!"

On college and high school campuses, students are forming prayer groups. *See You at the Pole* is a time when high school students, in spite of peer pressure or personal ridicule, make a stand for Christ by praying at the flagpole on campus before the beginning of the school year. From a few kids at first, thousands have now joined to affirm their faith. Young people are making a stand much like Daniel did in the court of Nebuchadnezzar.

Have you heard some of the latest reports?

"Prayer marches continue to grow both in numbers and participating cities. As of this writing nearly two million have been involved in one thousand cities, in forty-three countries."[18]

Since 1992, pastors in the New York metropolitan area have been meeting together in Pastor's Prayer Summits to seek God.

God is raising up people throughout this nation from all denominations, congregations, families, and individuals to pray for our country. Those who have studied the church's great "revivals" believe that wherever prayer increases, so do God's blessings.

Dr. Paul Cedar, president of the Evangelical Free Church of America, said, "Without a doubt the major opportunity before us is the potential of a historic revival, akin to the first and second Great Awakening. The encouraging sign of an impending awakening is the grass roots prayer movement God is raising up throughout this nation among individuals, parents, families, and congregations."

Billy Graham, speaking at the North American Conference for Itinerant Evangelists in June 1994, said, "So many prayer organizations have been set up . . . prayer summits and gatherings of people to pray—and great numbers for spiritual awakening . . . I think God is answering prayer and laying it upon the hearts of people so that when one preaches the gospel, like I do . . . it's easier to get people to respond today than it's ever been in the history of my work."

All of these stories suggest that we are standing on the threshold of what may be the most significant prayer movement of the church. The late Dr. Edwin Orr, in summarizing his sixty years of study on prayer and revival (earning him three Ph.D.s) said, "Whenever God is ready to do something with His people, He always sets them to praying."[19]

What's Happened Before Can Happen Again

"By the beginning of the eighteenth century the American churches had been overtaken by a creeping paralysis. The evangelical enthusiasm of the pioneering generation of colonists had not been maintained."[20]

Some ministers were bemoaning the worsening condition of churches and were calling for repentance when an earthquake in 1727 shook up New England and caused a temporary rush to the churches. (The same thing happened in California in 1994.) But there was very little lasting improvement. A Boston preacher said, "Alas, as though nothing but the most amazing thunders and lightnings, and the most terrible earthquakes could awaken us, we are at this time fallen into as dead a sleep as ever."[21]

Into this dry spirituality came George Whitefield, a pioneer in the English Revival. His first sermon in his native town of Gloucester, England, was of such fervor that someone complained to his bishop that he had driven fifteen people mad. The famous actor David Garrick once said, "I would give a hundred guineas if I could say 'Oh' like Mr. Whitefield."

When Whitefield visited America, he told the ministers in rather blunt language, "The reason why congregations have been so dead is because dead men preach to them."[22]

God raised up a powerful preacher, Jonathan Edwards, and the first Great Awakening spread from families to churches to towns. In his prolific writing, Edwards said, "The work of conversion was carried on in a most astonishing manner, and increased more and more; souls did come by flocks to Jesus Christ."[23]

In 1800, there were indications of a second Awakening. Camp meetings became popular tools of revival, and a great missionary movement spread here and abroad. Inspired by the evangelist Charles Finney and the founding of hundreds of church parish schools and colleges, America again saw Christian revivalism, this time linked with an increase in social concern.

The great spiritual awakenings that have taken place in our country were fueled by the fervent seeking after God of a few concerned souls. This is how it happened in the mid-1800s:

> In the middle of the nineteenth century, when our nation was divided over the issue of slavery, and people were living in a selfish, materialistic approach to life, God raised up Jeremiah Lamphier to lead a revival of prayer. In 1857, he began a prayer meeting in the upper room of the Old Fulton Street Dutch Reform Church in Manhattan. Beginning with only six people, the prayer meeting grew until the church was filled with praying people. By February of 1858, nearly ten thousand people a week were being converted. The impact of these prayer meetings spread from city to city across the United States. Cleveland, Detroit, Chicago, Cincinnati—city after city was conquered by the power of believing prayer.[24]

In 1982, I wrote, "The church today is cold, indifferent, and powerless. If we are to experience revival, there must be a new seeking after God with all our hearts and souls and minds."[25]

Now the signs of that revival are becoming stronger. Do you wonder that I want to shout, "What a great day to be alive!"?

Rejoice and beware. While we may reject the New Spirituality, we must also be cautious that the content of our own prayer and meditation is in the process of being conformed to the image of Christ.

Across the country we are hearing the repetition of a verse many people may not have recognized a decade ago. Whenever God addresses the subject of national change, He speaks primarily to His own people:

> If *my people* who are called by My name shall humble themselves, and pray and seek My face, and turn from their

wicked ways, then I will hear from heaven, and will forgive
their sin and heal their land. (2 Chron. 7:14, emphasis mine)

We are at a turning point in America. It was Howard
Hendricks who once said in a class at Dallas Seminary, "Deci-
sion determines direction, and direction determines destiny."
New Spirituality or biblical truth—which direction will we go?

13

ON THE
WINNING SIDE

WHEN I WAS PREACHING A MESSAGE on the New Age (before the New Spirituality became the current craze), one of my children asked, "Dad, what scary thing are you talking about tonight?"

I know some folks have wondered, is it *all* scary?

No! This is a great time to be alive! We are privileged to be a part of a generation that can see the prophetic scenario that foreshadows end-time events. But only a fool would stand before his congregation or write a book and say, "I am predicting that this is the final age."

Jesus said, "Heaven and earth will pass away, but My words will by no means pass away. But of that day and hour no one knows, not even the angels in heaven, nor the Son, but only the Father. Take heed, watch and pray; for you do not know when the time is" (Mark 13:31–33).

Jesus also said there would be a generation which would see all the signs unfold that would signal His soon return. One evidence would be a one-world government joined with a unified religious system. Both are on the horizon today.

In *Time* magazine, global unity is acclaimed, just as the Scriptures predict:

> The human drama, whether played out in history books or headlines, is often not just a confusing spectacle, but a

spectacle about confusion. The big question these days is which political forces will prevail: those that are stitching nations together or those that are tearing them apart? Here is one optimist's reason for believing unity will prevail over disunity, integration over disintegration. In fact, I'll bet that within the next 100 years nationhood as we know it today will be obsolete. *All states will recognize a single global authority.* (emphasis mine)[1]

Our global map is changing so fast that if you own one that was printed in the 1980s, it's obsolete today. Soon maps will be outdated before the colored ink is dry.

Our former president, George Bush, was the one man who probably has popularized the term *globalism* more than any other person in our generation. In a televised address to Congress on September 11, 1990, he said:

> A new partnership of nations has begun. We stand today at a unique and extraordinary moment. The crisis in the Persian Gulf, as grave as it is, also offers a rare opportunity to move toward an historic period of cooperation. Out of these troubled times, a new world order can emerge. A new era, freer from the threat of terror, stronger in pursuit of justice, and more secure in the quest for peace. . . .
>
> When we are successful, and we will be, we will have a new chance at this new world order, a world order in which a credible United Nations can use its peace keeping role to fulfill the promise and the vision of the United Nations' founders.

President Bush's advocacy of globalism is not based on any idea predicted in Scripture but comes from a genuine (but wrong) conviction that globalism is a solution to international warfare. As much as I admired President Bush, he was very mistaken about the United Nations' "peacekeeping role." If we believe that, we ignore the testimony of past history.

Racing Toward the New World Order

Globalists are not a well-defined, united group with identical ideas and/or goals. Some globalists may be mystical pantheists, some are economic or religious one-worlders, and others are centered on unity for ecological reasons.

The ecological arguments of Green Peace, the Club of Rome, the Sierra Club, and other groups say mankind must be the planetary steward of the world's ecology before the damage from pollution is irreversible. I can understand their concern because I live near the ocean in California. I have walked on the beaches out on the Silver Strand and have seen how pollution comes from the unsafe sewage systems in Mexico. While Donna and I were vacationing in Coronado, California, all the beaches were closed for three days during the peak of the tourist season because of pollution. Even after they opened, everyone was pretty wary about venturing into the surf.

The environmentalists say that when we have one world government, we will no longer have nations polluting other nations, because a world police force will be on the lookout for ecological hazards.

Actually, we are already one world technologically today. The global village establishment has millions of satellite-linked television sets linking us together by this gigantic eye in the sky. CNN has added a dimension to world events because the news is reported as it happens. All world leaders switch on CNN during times of crisis.

Globalism is promoted economically as the fluctuations of Wall Street are felt in London or Tokyo. At the same time, we are heading toward a cashless society where our financial privacy will be eliminated. Little plastic cards buy us everything from gasoline to bread, with further access to automatic check deposits and withdrawals. Before the advent of computers, this would have been impossible.

The scene has been set for the mark of the Beast when the Antichrist "causes all, both small and great, rich and poor, free and slave, to receive a mark on their right hand or on their foreheads, and that no one may buy or sell except one who has the mark or the name of the beast, or the number of his name" (Rev. 13:16–17).

One more reason given for this new world order is the fear-mongering that comes from the globalists. They say we have to come together or we will destroy ourselves. They warn of the danger to global peace by not having a global government.

But can you imagine replacing "God Bless America" with "We Are the World"?

Where Is This Leading?

I'm sure if you know anything about Bible prophecy you know that the Bible teaches that during the Tribulation there will be a man who is going to rule the world. He is the Antichrist.

In the early days of my ministry, I used to find it difficult to believe that such a person could ever have power over the whole world. But I don't think that anymore. In Daniel 7 and Revelation 13, this world ruler is described as a person with great charisma. He will be physically attractive, an outstanding orator, and a man of great cruelty. The Bible tells us he will have a spiritual bent as a cultic leader.

The global economy and false religious beliefs are setting the stage for this man to appear on the world scene and take control.

In recent years there have been many books written on the New Age movement. My friend Norman Geisler said, "One of the problems with much of the anti-New Age material is that it engenders more consciousness of the Antichrist than it does Christ. . . . We must be careful not to look for a demon on every doorknob or a spook of apostasy in every closet. This creates unnecessary suspicion in believers, from whose hearts God's love 'casts out fear, because fear involves torment'" (1 John 4:18).[2]

The point Geisler makes is valid. If Christ is our Lord and Savior, we do not need to linger in the darkness. Jesus said, "I am the Light of the world."

Our focus should be on Him, for it is written, "He who is in you is greater than he who is in the world" (1 John 4:4).

Christ versus Antichrist

If we are not careful we can dwell on the things that are going to happen in the end times and literally have our joy stolen from us. When we study prophecy and read about the events of our day, we should be able to walk away from that study with more hope in Christ than we have fear of the Antichrist.

I did not write this book to take away your hope. After all, "we have the prophetic word confirmed, which you do well to heed as a light that shines in a dark place, until the day dawns and the morning star rises in your hearts" (2 Pet. 1:19).

Life versus Death

We should not be living in fear of death. The New Testament Christian was not spending his time looking for the Antichrist; he was focusing on waiting for Christ. Paul reminded Titus that he was to be "looking for the blessed hope and glorious appearing of our God and Savior Jesus Christ" (Titus 2:13).

When I go on a trip, I am given an itinerary. Without it, I would be lost. Our God has given us a sequence of events in His timetable. According to the Scripture, the Antichrist will not be revealed until after the Rapture, when all true believers will be caught up to be with Jesus forever.[3] So if you are tuned into God, you will never have to worry about the Antichrist. You will be gone when he comes on the scene.

Since the events of prophecy cast their shadows before them, the Antichrist will surely be alive somewhere on the earth during the years preceding his appearance. However, too many people have faced embarrassment by saying that this person or that is the Antichrist. We don't know who he is; nor does anyone else.

I travel a great deal, and one of the things I hate to do is to leave Donna and my family. I love them very much and long to be with them. So as I return from a trip and my airplane approaches Lindbergh Field in San Diego, my heart starts to beat faster with anticipation. *Home at last!*

Someday you and I will reach our heavenly destination. Jesus will either take us there before we die physically or He will be waiting when the doctor bends over us and says, "It's over." Either way we will be *home at last!*

Great Day versus Doomsday

Those of us who speak or write about biblical prophecy are sometimes labeled as "Doomsdayers." It's the newswriters and futurists who should have that label. It's true that the Bible predicts a great time of war and tribulation coming. But it also says this is going to be followed by a time of eternal peace. Things are going to get worse before they get better, but we have no reason to get discouraged because the Lord God is going to make sure every believer is saved from the hour of wrath.

One of the great verses for those of us who are pre-Tribulationists is, "There is therefore now no condemnation to those who are in Christ Jesus" (Rom. 8:1).

The period of Tribulation is going to be short, but we are not going to be here to experience its horror. We will be with Almighty God for eternity. Knowing this, we can be eternal optimists!

Good News versus Gloom News

My co-author and I have felt the oppression of studying about the New Spirituality, but we do not want to be consumed by it. We are going to walk away from this research, knowing that the information is there if we need it. We hope that you are more sensitive now to what's going on in the world around us.

I don't want to run around cursing the darkness. That's not what God has called me to do. The gospel is *good* news. When the Bible speaks about the coming of the Lord, it says, "Therefore comfort one another with these words" (1 Thess. 4:18). Think of the word *comfort* as *encourage*.

God has prepared a wonderful and glorious future for all who name the name of Christ in faith.

The next great event is not the coming of the Antichrist. It is the Great Escape.

> For the Lord Himself will descend from heaven with a shout, with the voice of an archangel, and with the trumpet of God. And the dead in Christ will rise first. Then we who are alive and remain shall be caught up together with

...ord in the air. And thus
... (1 Thess. 4:16–17)

...o have a false hope in the ...ivated by love and compas-...us Christ, the hope of the

...and emptiness like the Lord ...1 while there's still time! If ...you can put down this book ...onfess that I am a sinner. I ...be my Savior."

...1 the words, He listens and ...He will never leave us or for-

...ound with our heads down. We can get caught up with the dismal predictions of the New Spirituality and get lost.

The important thing to remember is this: Christ has already defeated Satan and all of his host at the cross. Satan's power is limited, hedged in by the sovereign God. God is in charge!

The events that are going on down here may stress us out, but God knows how they are going to end. If we read the Book, we should know too.

In an athletic contest, the celebration sometimes begins too soon. My sons are both football players, so we see a lot of games. I remember one game we watched where our coach taught the guys a great lesson. We had scored the touchdown that put us ahead, 21 to 17. Our kids got carried away, jumping up and down and celebrating. Everyone was high-fiving everyone else.

The coach got those guys in a circle, and I'll never forget what he said. "The game isn't over!" he told them. "I don't want any celebrating until the last gun goes off. Get yourselves under control."

I thought about that as I looked over all of these chapters. I know we're going to win, but the game isn't over yet. The celebration is coming, but in the meantime, I have to keep myself under control. When we get to glory, I'll high-five with the best of you because I know what a great celebration it's going to be!

We are on our way to the victory party! We can live in anticipation of winning the homecoming game. But let's not fall into Satan's ditch before we get there!

Notes

Introduction

1. Barbara Kantrowitz and others, *Newsweek*, 28 November 1994, 53.
2. Herbert Schlossberg, *Idols for Destruction* (New York: Thomas Nelson, 1983), 233.
3. Ibid., 234.
4. Andres Tapia, "Reaching the First Post-Christian," *Christianity Today*, 12 September 1994, 22.

Chapter 1   The Snare of the Savage Wolves

1. John Naisbitt and Patricia Aburdene, *Megatrends 2000* (New York: William Morrow, 1990), 280.
2. Dick Sutphen, "Infiltrating the New Age into Society," *What Is*, vol. 1, no. 1, cited in Eric Buehrer, *The New Age Masquerade* (Brentwood, Tenn.: Wolgemuth & Hyatt Publishers Inc. 1990), 69.
3. Marilyn Ferguson, *The Aquarian Conspiracy* (Los Angeles: J. P. Tarcher, 1980), 23.
4. "Celestial Reasoning," *People*, 25 April 1994, 86.
5. James Redfield, *The Celestine Prophecy* (New York: Warner, 1993), 98.
6. Shirley MacLaine, *Out on a Limb* (New York: Bantam, 1983), 333.
7. David Jeremiah with C. C. Carlson, *The Handwriting on the Wall* (Dallas: Word, 1992), 242.
8. "Spiritual America," *People*, 4 April 1994, 48.
9. Ibid., 50.
10. M. Scott Peck, M.D., *Further Along the Road Less Traveled* (New York: Simon and Schuster, 1993), 155.

11. *The American Heritage Dictionary* (New York: Dell, 1983).
12. Joseph Smith, *History of the Church* (Salt Lake City: Deseret Books), 6:305–6.
13. J. D. Salinger, *Nine Stories* (New York: Bantam, 1971), 189.
14. Brian O'Leary, Ph.D., "When the Paranormal and Science Meet," *Body Mind Spirit,* May/June 1994, 31.

Chapter 2   Invasion from the East

1. Beverly Beyette, "Color This Peaceful," *Los Angeles Times,* 12 August 1994, E-4.
2. "Healing with History," *San Diego Union-Tribune,* 18 November 1994, E1.
3. Mark S. Hoffman, editor, *The World Almanac 1993* (New York: Pharos Books), 718.
4. Edward Rice, *Eastern Definitions* (Garden City, N.Y.: Doubleday, 1978), 166–67.
5. Kurt Friedrichs, "Hinduism," in Stephan Schumacher, Gert Woerner, editors, *The Encylopedia of Eastern Philosophy and Religion* (Boston: Shambhala, 1989), 130.
6. John Ankerberg and John Weldon, *The Facts on Hinduism in America* (Eugene, Ore.: Harvest House, 1991), 7.
7. Ibid., 9.
8. From David L. Johnson, *A Reasoned Look at Asian Religions* (Minneapolis: Bethany House, 1985), 105.
9. Ibid., 107.
10. John Weldon with Zola Levitt, *The Transcendental Explosion* (Irvine, Calif.: Harvest House, 1976), 15.
11. Ibid., 195.
12. Ibid., 19.
13. See Ankerberg and Weldon, *The Facts on Hinduism in América,* 9.
14. Ibid., 19–20.
15. C. S. Lewis, *The Problem of Pain* (New York: Macmillan, 1962), 150–51.
16. Ankerberg and Weldon, *The Facts on Hinduism in America,* 21.
17. Ibid., 20.
18. Ibid, 21.
19. Cited in F. LaGard Smith, *Out On a Broken Limb* (Eugene, Ore.: Harvest House, 1986), 181.

20. Caryl Matriciano, *Gods of the New Age* (Eugene, Ore.: Harvest House, 1985), 136.

Chapter 3   Many Happy (?) Returns

1. From a booklet published by the Unarius Academy of Science, El Cajon, California, 1992, 15.
2. Ibid.
3. Norman L. Geisler and J. Yutaka Amano, *The Reincarnation Sensation* (Wheaton, Ill.: Tyndale House, 1986), 7–8.
4. Tiffany Porter, "Therapists find cures are matter of lives and deaths," *San Diego Union-Tribune,* 20 August 1993, E1–3.
5. Ibid.
6. Ibid.
7. "India: Religion and Philosophy," *Encyclopedia Americana* (Danbury, Conn.: Grolier, 1986), 870.
8. Cited in Geisler and Amano, *Reincarnation Sensation.*
9. Caryl Matriciano, *Gods of the New Age* (Eugene, Ore.: Harvest House, 1985), 44.
10. "The Best Year of Her Lives," *Time,* 14 May 1984, 62.
11. J. Gordon Melton, *New Age Encyclopedia* (Detroit, New York, and London: Gale Research, 1990), 299.
12. Cited in Geisler and Amano, *The Reincarnation Sensation,* 25–26.
13. *Newsweek,* 28 November 1994, 54.
14. Billy Graham, *Facing Death and the Life After* (Minneapolis: Grason, 1987), 52.
15. Rosalind Wright, "Love, Death, and Terri Hoffman," *Good Housekeeping,* October 1990, 62.

Chapter 4   The Force

1. George Barna, *Baby Busters, the Disillusioned Generation* (Chicago: Northfield Publishing, 1992), 143–44.
2. C. S. Lewis, *The Screwtape Letters* (New York: MacMillan, 1961), 32–33.
3. Ankerberg and Weldon, *The Facts on the New Age Movement* (Eugene, Ore.: Harvest House, 1988), 35.
4. *McCall's,* March 1989, 69.
5. Lynn Smith, "The New, Chic Metaphysical Fad of Channeling," *Los Angeles Times,* 5 December 1986, Part V.

6. *Newsweek,* 28 November 1994, 59

7. Ibid.

8. Betsy Pisik, "Opening a Direct Channel through the Metaphysical," *Washington Times,* 5 February 1992, E-4.

9. Craig Lee, "Messages from Channel Infinity," *Los Angeles Weekly,* 7–13 November 1986, 20.

10. Carol M. Ostrom, "Tuning in on the Master's Channel," *Seattle Times,* 5 June 1983, Section D.

11. "Ramtha—An Exclusive Interview with His Channel, J. Z. Knight," *Holistic Life Magazine,* Summer 1985, 30.

12. See "Heeeeres's Ramtha," *New Age Journal,* June 1986, 12.

13. Allan Spraggett, *The Unexplained* (New York: New American Library, 1967), 65.

14. George Hackett with Pamela Adamson, "Ramtha, A Voice from Beyond," *Newsweek,* December 1986, 42.

15. John Ankerberg and John Weldon, *The Facts on Spirit Guides* (Eugene, Ore.: Harvest House, 1988), 16.

Chapter 5   Rescue Our Captive Children

1. Bob and Gretchen Passantino, *When the Devil Dares Your Kids* (Ann Arbor, Mich.: Servant, 1991), 126.

2. Quoted in Berit Kjos, *Your Child and the New Age* (Wheaton, Ill.: Victor, 1990), 115.

3. Ibid., 122.

4. Ibid., 123.

5. Story taken from Neil T. Anderson and Steve Russo, *The Seduction of Our Children* (Eugene, Ore.: Harvest House, 1991), 75.

6. Kjos, *Your Child and the New Age,* 121.

7. Anderson and Russo, *The Seduction of Our Children,* 103.

8. David Jeremiah with Carole C. Carlson, *Exposing the Myths of Parenthood* (Dallas: Word, 1988), 88–89.

Chapter 6   Schools Under Siege

1. "Adult Literacy in America," National Center for Educational Statistics, U.S. Dept. of Education, 555 New Jersey Ave., N.W., Washington, D.C., September 1993.

2. John Dunphy, "A Religion for a New Age," *The Humanist,* January/February 1983, 26. Quoted in Berit Kjos, *Your Child and the New Age,* 18.

3. Marilyn Ferguson, *The Aquarian Conspiracy* (Los Angeles: Tarcher, 1980), 280–81.
4. Kjos, *Your Child and the New Age*, 17.
5. Eric Buehrer, *The New Age Masquerade* (Brentwood, Tenn.: Wolgemuth and Hyatt, 1990), 97.
6. Telephone interview by C. C. Carlson with Eric Buehrer, 2 August 1994.
7. Anne Carson, *Spiritual Parenting in the New Age* (Freedom, Calif.: The Crossing Press, 1989), 153.
8. Eric Buehrer explores this concept in his series of booklets, *How To Be Sure Your Child Is Safe from the New Age*, from Gateways to Better Education, P.O. Box 514, Lake Forest, California 92630.
9. Carson, *Spiritual Parenting*, 159.
10. Frances Adeney, "Educators Look East," *SCP Journal* (Winter 1981–82), 28. Quoted by Erwin W. Lutzer and John F. DeVries, *Satan's Evangelistic Strategy for the New Age* (Wheaton, Ill.: Scripture Press, 1989), 137.
11. Philip Vander Velde and Hyung-Chan Kim, editors., *Global Mandate: Pedagogy for Peace* (Bellingham, Wash.: Bellwether, 1985), 351.
12. Ibid., *Global Mandate*, 10.
13. For further information see Buehrer, *New Age Masquerade*, 110–11.
14. Fritjof Capra, *The Turning Point* (New York: Simon and Schuster, 1982), 78.
15. William Bowen Jr., *Globalism: America's Demise* (Lafayette, La.: Huntington House, 1984), 131. Quoted in Lutzer and DeVries, *Satan's Evangelistic Strategy for the New Age*, 151.
16. Al Gore, *Earth in the Balance* (New York: Houghton Mifflin, 1992), 259.
17. National Association of Christian Educators and Citizens for Excellence in Education, P.O. Box 3200, Costa Mesa, California 92628, and Gateways to Better Education, P. O. Box 514, Lake Forest, California 92630.
18. Dr. Thomas Sowell, "Indoctrinating the Children," *Forbes*, 1 February 1993, 65.

Chapter 7 Crystal Clear

1. *Parade Magazine*, 21 October 1990.
2. *Parade Magazine*, 5 August 1990.
3. *Time*, 19 January 1987, 66.

4. Brett Bravo, *Crystal Healing Secrets* (New York: Warner, 1988), 13.
5. Ibid., 12.
6. Ibid., 107.
7. "Crazy over Crystals," *Los Angeles Herald Examiner*, 18 January 1987.
8. Ibid., 22–23.
9. Ibid.
10. *Los Angeles Times*, 29 August 1994.
11. 2 Timothy 4:1–4 in Eugene H. Peterson, *The Message, The New Testament in Contemporary Language* (Colorado Springs: Navpress, 1993), 449.

Chapter 8   New Gods in the Waiting Room

1. Special thanks to Janice Lyons, director of *Current Issues in Alternative Medicine*, published in Asheville, North Carolina, for her research on these issues.
2. Paul C. Reisser, M.D., Teri K. Reisser, John Weldon, *New Age Medicine* (Downers Grove, Ill.: InterVarsity, 1987), 9.
3. Samuel Pfeifer, M.D., *Healing . . . At Any Price?* (Milton Keynes, England: Word, 1988), Introduction.
4. *San Diego Magazine*, November 1993, 78.
5. Deepak Chopra, *Ageless Body, Timeless Mind* (New York: Harmony Books, 1993), 269.
6. *Los Angeles Times*, 19 September 1994, A–3.
7. Ibid.
8. *San Diego Magazine*, November 1993.
9. Ibid.
10. Bernie S. Siegel, M.D., *Love, Medicine, and Miracles* (New York: Harper and Row, 1986), 19–20.
11. *The Tao* is the ancient Chinese philosophical system that expounds the concept of "the way," an impersonal concept of ultimate reality. "Taoism is centered on the importance of process and change, the concept that nature and the universe flow in an endless course of continuous cycles. Taoism urges human beings, who are seen as utterly dependent on nature, to live in harmony with these cycles and thus be 'one' with the Tao. The person who does so is promised success and long life, while the person who 'bucks the system' of nature will suffer failure, disease and an early grave." (From Reisser, Reisser,

and Weldon, *New Age Medicine*). *Yin and Yang* is an ancient system of Chinese medicine based on the principle that health is achieved by balancing *yin* and *yang* energies in the body. They are opposite polarities, *yin* being regarded traditionally as passive, negative, and feminine, and *yang* as active, positive, and masculine. *The five therapies*: First, the treatment of the spirit, the practice of a tranquil way of life. Second and third, dietary and medicinal therapies, fourth is acupuncture, and the fifth is massage.

12. Samuel Pfeifer, M.D., *Healing . . . At Any Price?* 29.
13. Reisser, Reisser, and Weldon, *New Age Medicine*, 52.
14. Edward C. Hamlyn, M.D., *The Healing Art of Homeopathy* (New Canaan, Conn.: Keats Publishing, 1979), 15.
15. John Ankerberg and John Weldon, *The Facts on Holistic Health and the New Medicine* (Eugene, Ore.: Harvest House, 1992).
16. Bob Larson, *Straight Answers on the New Age* (Nashville: Thomas Nelson, 1989), 62.
17. Christian Chiropractors Association (P.O. Box 9715, Fort Collins, Colorado 80525-0500), vol. XXIX, December 1988.
18. Telephone interview with the Rev. Roland Murphy, 17 November 1994.
19. Reisser, Reisser, and Weldon, *New Age Medicine*, 15.
20. Richard Svihus, "The Concept of Holistic Health: Origins and Definitions," in *The Journal of Holistic Health* (San Diego: Association for Holistic Health, 1977), 17. Quoted in Reisser, Reisser, and Weldon, *New Age Medicine*, 16.

Chapter 9 Corporate Takeovers

1. Richard Bach, *Jonathan Livingston Seagull* (New York: Macmillan, 1970), 27.
2. Reply from Professor Drucker, fall 1994.
3. Tal Brooke, *When the World Will Be As One* (Eugene, Ore.: Harvest House, 1989), 91.
4. Anthony Robbins, *Awakening the Giant Within* (New York: Simon and Schuster, 1991), 108.
5. Walter Martin, *The New Cults* (Santa Ana, Calif.: Vision House, 1980), 106.
6. *Spiritual Fitness in Business*, Probe Ministries International, Richardson, Texas, March, 1989

7. Tal Brooke, "Gates of Entry for the Occult," *Spiritual Counter-feits Project Journal*, vol. 9, no. 1 (1989).
8. Ibid.
9. *Spiritual Fitness in Business*, Probe Ministries International, Richardson, Texas, March 1989.
10. Brooke, "Gates of Entry for the Occult."
11. *Los Angeles Times*, 15 August 1988, V1.
12. Jeremy Main, "Trying to Bend Managers' Minds," *Fortune*, 23 November 1987, 104.
13. Robert Lindsey, "Gurus Hired to Motivate Workers are Raising Fears of 'Mind Control,'" *New York Times*, 17 April 1987.
14. "Angels, Ecology, and Comfort," *Sportscast*, Spring and Summer 1994.
15. Bob Ortega, "Research Institute Shows People a Way Out of Their Bodies," *Wall Street Journal*, 20 September 1994.
16. A. W. Tozer, source unknown.
17. C. S. Lewis, *God in the Dock: Essays on Theology and Ethics* (Grand Rapids, Mich.: William W. Eerdmans, 1970), 93.

Chapter 10   Spirit Guides on the Bookshelves

1. *Publisher's Weekly*, 6 December 1993.
2. Nancy Gibbs, "Angels Among Us," *Time*, 27 December 1993.
3. *Southern California Christian Times*, March 1994.
4. Betty Eadie, *Embraced by the Light* (New York: Bantam, 1994), 45.
5. Ibid., 47.
6. Ibid., 50.
7. Ibid., 47.
8. PBS special, *In Search of Angels*, on Los Angeles station KCET, 14 August 1994.
9. Eileen Freeman, *Touched by Angels* (New York: Warner, 1993), 155.
10. Ibid., 64.
11. Billy Graham, *Angels* (New York: Doubleday & Company, 1975), 94.
12. Ibid., 95.
13. Ibid., 139.
14. Marianne Williamson, *A Return to Love* (New York: HarperCollins, 1992), 29.
15. Ibid., 38.

16. Ibid., 29.
17. Ibid., 18, 34.
18. Paul Elie, "Horizon 2000," *Publisher's Weekly*, 7 December 1992.

Chapter 11   Goddess of Mother Earth

1. Francis Schaeffer, *Pollution and the Death of Man . . . The Christian View of Ecology* (Wheaton, Ill.: Tyndale House, 1970), 12.
2. Ibid.
3. Tal Brooke, "The Ecological Great Awakening: Earthcrisis and Eco-purges," *Spiritual Counterfeits Project Journal*, vol. 1 (Berkeley, Calif., 1992), 7:3, 8
4. Knight-Ridder News Service, 23 April 1990.
5. Sam Keen, *Hymns to an Unknown God* (New York: Bantam, 1994), xix.
6. Ibid., 215.
7. Barry McWaters, *Conscious Evolution* (Los Angeles: New Age Press, 1981), xii, from the foreword by David Spangler.
8. Carl Sagan, "To Avert a Common Danger," *Parade Magazine*, 1 March 1992.
9. *A Constitution for the Federation of the Earth* (Lakewood, Colo.: World Constitution and Parliament Association, 1991).
10. Edward C. Wolf, "Avoiding a Mass Extinction of the Species," *State of the World* (New York: Norton, 1988), 114.
11. Cited by Tim Stafford, "Are People the Problem?" *Christianity Today*, 3 October 1994, 49.
12. Charles Westoff, "Fertility in the United States," *Science Magazine*, October 1986.
13. Ben J. Wattenbert, *The Birth Dearth* (New York: Pharos Books, 1987), 170–71.
14. George Grant, *The Legacy of Planned Parenthood* (Brentwood, Tenn.: Wolgemuth & Hyatt), 26, excerpted from *Grand Illusions: The Legacy of Planned Parenthood*. Also see Planned Parenthood Federation of America's *Federation Declaration of Principles*, 1980.
15. Ibid.
16. See Grant's documentation in *Grand Illusion: The Legacy of Planned Parenthood*, 17.
17. Gore, *Earth in the Balance*, 161–62.

18. Doug Groothuis, "American's Ecological Millennium . . . Al Gore in the Balance," *SCP Journal*, vol. 17, no. 3 (1992): 32.
19. *The Wichita Eagle*, 22 February 1992, Religion and Ethics Section.
20. Lynn White, "The Historic Roots of Our Ecologic Crisis," *Science* (1967): 155:1203–7.
21. Jonathan Porritt, *Seeing Green* (Oxford: Blackwell, 1986), quoted in *SCP Journal*, vol. 17, no. 3 (1992), 211.
22. Dr. Eugene Taylor, "Desperately Seeking Spirituality," *Psychology Today*, November/December 1994.
23. *Azusa Pacific Life*, Spring 1994.
24. Schaeffer, *Pollution and the Death of Man*, 93.

Chapter 12   Inside the Church Door

1. *Newsweek*, 6 January 1992.
2. Ibid.
3. Martin Marty, quoted by Timothy Jones, "Great Awakenings," *Christianity Today*, 8 November 1993.
4. Albert James Dager, *Inner Healing . . . A Biblical Analysis*, (Costa Mesa, Calif.: Media Spotlight, 1986).
5. Ibid., 9.
6. Agnes Sanford, *The Healing Gifts of the Spirit* (Old Tappan, N.J.: Spire Books by Fleming Revell, 1982), 27.
7. Ibid., 53.
8. Dager, *Inner Healing, a Biblical Analysis*, 56–57.
9. Roy Rivenburg, "Faith or Fad?" *Los Angeles Times*, 17 April 1994, E1.
10. Ibid.
11. Ibid.
12. *Spiritual Counterfeits Project Newsletter*, Winter 1993.
13. David Crumm, "Bible Isn't Jesus' Gospel Truth, Scholars Say," *Orange County Register*, 12 December 1993.
14. *The San Diego Union-Tribune*, 17 October 1994.
15. "Faith in our Time," *Santa Barbara News Press*, 16 October 1994.
16. Eugene Peterson, "Spirit Quest," *Christianity Today*, 8 November 1993.
17. Interview with General Abel, 27 October 1994.
18. David Bryant, "An Amazing Prayer Movement Signals Hope for World Revival," *World Evangelization Magazine*, September/October 1994.

19. Ibid.
20. *Eerdmans' Handbook to The History of Christianity*, (Berkhamsted, Herts, England: Lion Publishing, 1977, Guideposts edition), 436.
21. Ibid.
22. Ibid., 441.
23. Ibid., 439.
24. Jerry Falwell, *Listen America* (Garden City, N.Y.: Doubleday, 1980), 246–47.
25. David Jeremiah, *Before It's Too Late* (Nashville: Thomas Nelson, 1982), 172.

Chapter 13   On the Winning Side

1. Strobe Talbott, "The Birth of the Global Nation," *Time*, 20 July 1992, 70–71.
2. Norman Geisler and J. Yutaka Amano, *The Infiltration of the New Age* (Wheaton, Ill.: Tyndale House, 1989), 95.
3. A pre-Tribulational view is that all true believers in Jesus Christ will be "raptured" before the beginning of the Tribulation (see Thess. 4:16–17).

SUBJECT INDEX

SCRIPTURE INDEX